Religions
of the
World

BUDDHISM

CHRISTIANITY

CONFUCIANISM

HINDUISM

ISLAM

JUDAISM

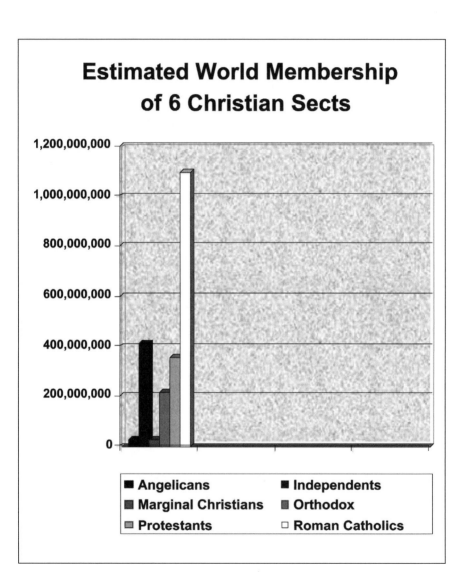

Estimated World Membership of 6 Christian Sects

RELIGIONS
OF THE
WORLD

CHRISTIANITY

Ann Marie B. Bahr

Series Consulting Editor Ann Marie B. Bahr
Professor of Religious Studies,
South Dakota State University

Foreword by Martin E. Marty
Professor Emeritus,
University of Chicago Divinity School

CHELSEA HOUSE
PUBLISHERS
A Haights Cross Communications Company
Philadelphia

FRONTIS This chart shows the estimated world membership of six of the largest Christian denominations. It is based on information from the International Bulletin of Missionary Research, published in January 2003.

CHELSEA HOUSE PUBLISHERS

VP, NEW PRODUCT DEVELOPMENT Sally Cheney
DIRECTOR OF PRODUCTION Kim Shinners
CREATIVE MANAGER Takeshi Takahashi
MANUFACTURING MANAGER Diann Grasse

Staff for CHRISTIANITY

EXECUTIVE EDITOR Lee Marcott
SENIOR EDITOR Tara Koellhoffer
PRODUCTION EDITOR Megan Emery
ASSISTANT PHOTO EDITOR Noelle Nardone
SERIES AND COVER DESIGNER Keith Trego
LAYOUT 21st Century Publishing and Communications, Inc.

A Haights Cross Communications ⌐ Company

www.chelseahouse.com

First Printing

9 8 7 6 5 4 3 2 1

Library of Congress Cataloging-in-Publication Data

Bahr, Ann Marie B.
  Christianity / Ann Marie B. Bahr.
    v. cm. — (Religions of the world)
  Includes bibliographical references and index.
  Contents: Jesus of Nazareth — Scriptures — Worldview — Visiting
  Christian churches — Growing up Christian — Christian cultural
  expressions — Calendar and holidays — History — Christianity in the
  world today.
  ISBN 0-7910-7856-6
  1. Christianity—Juvenile literature. [1. Christianity.] I. Title.
II. Series. BR125.5.B34 2003 230—dc22
                          2003023918

CONTENTS

Foreword

On this very day, like all other days, hundreds of millions of people around the world will turn to religion for various purposes.

On the one hand, there are purposes that believers in any or all faiths, as well as unbelievers, might regard as positive and benign. People turn to religion or, better, to their own particular faith, for the experience of healing and to inspire acts of peacemaking. They want to make sense of a world that can all too easily overwhelm them because it so often seems to be meaningless and even absurd. Religion then provides them with beauty, inspires their souls, and impels them to engage in acts of justice and mercy.

To be informed citizens of our world, readers have good reason to learn about these features of religions that mean so much to so many. Those who study the faiths do not have to agree with any of them and could not agree with all of them, different as they are. But they need basic knowledge of religions to understand other people and to work out strategies for living with them.

On the other hand—and religions always have an "other hand"—believers in any of the faiths, and even unbelievers who are against all of them, will find their fellow humans turning to their religions for purposes that seem to contradict all those positive features. Just as religious people can heal and be healed, they can also kill or be killed in the name of faith. So it has been through history.

This killing can be literal: Most armed conflicts and much terrorism today are inspired by the stories, commands, and promises that come along with various faiths. People can and do read and act upon scriptures that can breed prejudice and that lead them to reject other beliefs and believers. Or the killing can be figurative, which means that faiths can be deadening to the spirit. In the name of faith, many people are repressed, oppressed, sometimes victimized and abused.

If religion can be dangerous and if it may then come with "Handle with Care" labels, people who care for their own security, who want to lessen tensions and inspire concord, have to equip themselves by learning something about the scriptures and stories of their own and other faiths. And if they simply want to take delight in human varieties and imaginings, they will find plenty to please them in lively and reliable accounts of faiths.

A glance at television or at newspapers and magazines on almost any day will reveal stories that display one or both sides of religion. However, these stories usually have to share space with so many competing accounts, for example, of sports and entertainment or business and science, that writers and broadcasters can rarely provide background while writing headlines. Without such background, it is hard to make informed judgments.

The series RELIGIONS OF THE WORLD is designed to provide not only background but also rich illustrative material about the foreground, presenting the many features of faiths that are close at hand. Whoever reads all six volumes will find that these religions have some elements in common. Overall, one can deduce that their followers take certain things with ultimate seriousness: human dignity, devotion to the sacred, the impulse to live a moral life. Yet few people are inspired by religions in general. They draw strength from what they hold particularly. These particulars of each faith are not always contradictory to those of others, but they are different in important ways. It is simply a fact that believers are informed and inspired by stories told in separate and special ways.

A picture might make all this vivid: Reading about a religion, visiting a place of worship, or coming into the company of those who believe in and belong to a particular faith, is like entering a room. Religions are, in a sense, spiritual "furnished apartments." Their adherents have placed certain pictures on the wall and moved in with their own kind of furnishings, having developed their special ways of receiving or blocking out light from such places. Some of their figurative apartments are airy, and some stress strength and security.

Philosopher George Santayana once wrote that, just as we do not speak language, we speak particular languages, so we have religion not as a whole but as religions "in particular." The power of each living and healthy religion, he added, consists in "its special and surprising message and in the bias which that revelation gives to life." Each creates "another world to live in."

The volumes in this series are introductions to several spiritual furnished apartments, guides to the special and surprising messages of these large and complex communities of faith, or religions. These are not presented as a set of items in a cafeteria line down which samplers walk, tasting this, rejecting that, and moving on. They are not bids for window-shoppers or shoppers of any sort, though it may be that a person without faith might be drawn to one or another expression of the religions here described. The real intention of the series is to educate.

Education could be dull and drab. Picture a boring professor standing in front of a class and droning on about distant realities. The authors in this series, however, were chosen because they can bring readers up close to faiths and, sometimes better, to people of faith; not to religion but to people who are religious in particular ways.

As one walks the streets of a great metropolis, it is not easy and may not even be possible to deduce what are the faith-commitments of those one passes unless they wear a particular costume, some garb or symbol prescribed by their faith. Therefore, while passing them by, it is not likely that one can learn much about the dreams and hopes, the fears and intentions, of those around them.

These books, in effect, stop the procession of passersby and bid visitors to enter those sanctuaries where communities worship. Each book could serve as a guide to worship. Several years ago, a book called *How to Be a Perfect Stranger* offered brief counsel on how to feel and to be at home among worshipers from other traditions. This series recognizes that we are not strangers to each other only in sanctuaries. We carry over our attachments to conflicting faiths where we go to work or vote or serve in the military or have fun. These "carryovers" tend to come from the basic stories and messages of the several faiths.

The publishers have taken great pains to assign their work to authors of a particular sort. Had these been anti-religious or anti–the religion about which they write, they would have done a disservice. They would, in effect, have been blocking the figurative doors to the faiths or smashing the furniture in the sanctuaries. On the other hand, it would be wearying and distorting had the assignment gone to public relations agents, advertisers who felt called to claim "We're Number One!" concerning the faith about which they write.

Fair-mindedness and accuracy are the two main marks of these authors. In rather short compass, they reach a wide range of subjects, focusing on everything one needs to advance basic understanding. Their books are like mini-encyclopedias, full of information. They introduce the holidays that draw some neighbors to be absent from work or school for a day or a season. They include galleries of notable figures in each faith-community.

Since most religions in the course of history develop different ways in the many diverse places where they thrive, or because they attract intelligent, strong-willed leaders and writers, they come up with different emphases. They divide and split off into numberless smaller groups: Protestant and Catholic and Orthodox Christians, Shiite and Sunni Muslims, Orthodox and Reform Jews, and many kinds of Buddhists and Hindus. The writers in this series do justice to these variations, providing a kind of map without which one will get lost in the effort to understand.

Some years ago, a rabbi friend, Samuel Sandmel, wrote a book about his faith called *The Enjoyment of Scriptures*. What an astonishing concept, some might think: After all, religious scriptures deal with desperately urgent, life-and-death-and-eternity issues. They have to be grim and those who read them likewise. Not so. Sandmel knew what the authors of this series also know and impart: that the journeys of faith and the encounter with the religions of others include pleasing and challenging surprises. I picture many a reader coming across something on these pages that at first looks obscure or forbidding, but then, after a slightly longer look, makes sense and inspires an "aha!" There are many occasions for "aha-ing!" in these books. One can also wager that many a reader will come away from the encounters thinking, "I never knew that!" or "I never thought of that before." And they will be more ready than they had been to meet strangers of other faiths in a world that so many faiths *have* to share, or that they *get* to share.

Martin E. Marty
The University of Chicago

Preface

The majority of people, both in the United States and around the world, consider religion to be an important part of their lives. Beyond its significance in individual lives, religion also plays an important role in war and peace, politics, social policy, ethics, and cultural expression. Yet few people feel well-prepared to carry on a conversation about religion with friends, colleagues, or their congressional delegation. The amount of knowledge people have about their own faith varies, but very few can lay claim to a solid understanding of a religion other than their own. As the world is drawn closer together by modern communications, and the religions of the world jostle each other in religiously plural societies, the lack of our ability to dialogue about this aspect of our lives results in intercultural conflict rather than cooperation. It means that individuals of different religious persuasions will either fight about their faiths or avoid the topic of religion altogether. Neither of these responses aids in the building of healthy, religiously plural societies. This gap in our knowledge is therefore significant, and grows increasingly more significant as religion plays a larger role in national and international politics.

The authors and editors of this series are dedicated to the task of helping to prepare present and future decision-makers to deal with religious pluralism in a healthy way. The objective scholarship found in these volumes will blunt the persuasive power of popular misinformation. The time is short, however. Even now, nations are dividing along religious lines, and "neutral" states as well as partisan religious organizations are precariously, if not always intentionally, tipping delicate balances of power in favor of one religious group or another with doles of aid and support for certain policies or political leaders. Intervention in the affairs of other nations is always a risky business, but doing it without understanding of the religious sensitivities of the populace dramatically increases the chances that even well-intentioned intervention will be perceived as political coercion or cultural invasion. With such signs of ignorance already manifest, the day of reckoning for educational policies that ignore the study of the world's religions cannot be far off.

This series is designed to bring religious studies scholarship to the leaders of today and tomorrow. It aims to answer the questions that students, educators, policymakers, parents, and citizens might have about the new religious milieu in which we find ourselves. For example, a person hearing about a religion that is foreign to him or her might want answers to questions like these:

- How many people believe in this religion? What is its geographic distribution? When, where, and how did it originate?

- What are its beliefs and teachings? How do believers worship or otherwise practice their faith?

- What are the primary means of social reinforcement? How do believers educate their youth? What are their most important communal celebrations?

- What are the cultural expressions of this religion? Has it inspired certain styles of art, architecture, literature, or music? Conversely, does it avoid art, literature, or music for religious reasons? Is it associated with elements of popular culture?

- How do the people who belong to this religion remember the past? What have been the most significant moments in their history?

- What are the most salient features of this religion today? What is likely to be its future?

We have attempted to provide as broad coverage as possible of the various religious forces currently shaping the planet. Judaism, Christianity, Islam, Hinduism, Buddhism, Confucianism, Taoism, Sikhism, and Shinto have each been allocated an entire volume. In recognition of the fact that many smaller ancient and new traditions also exercise global influence, we present coverage of some of these in two additional volumes titled "Tribal Religions" and "New Religions." Each volume in the series discusses demographics and geography, founder or foundational period, scriptures, worldview, worship or practice, growing up in the religion, cultural expressions, calendar and holidays, history, and the religion in the world today.

The books in this series are written by scholars. Their approach to their subject matter is neutral and objective. They are not trying to convert readers to the religion they are describing. Most scholars, however, value the religion they have chosen to study, so you can expect the general tone of these books to be appreciative rather than critical.

Religious studies scholars are experts in their field, but they are not critics in the same sense in which one might be an art, film, or literary critic. Religious studies scholars feel obligated to describe a tradition faithfully and accurately, and to interpret it in a way that will allow nonbelievers as well as believers to grasp its essential structure, but they do not feel compelled to pass judgment on it. Their goal is to increase knowledge and understanding.

Academic writing has a reputation for being dry and uninspiring. If so, religious studies scholarship is an exception. Scholars of religion have the happy task of describing the words and deeds of some of the world's most amazing people: founders, prophets, sages, saints, martyrs, and bodhisattvas.

The power of religion moves us. Today, as in centuries past, people thrill to the ethical vision of Confucianism, or the dancing beauty of Hinduism's images of the divine. They are challenged by the one, holy God of the Jews, and comforted by the saving promise of Christianity. They are inspired by the stark purity of

Islam, by the resilience of tribal religions, by the energy and innovation of the new religions. The religions have retained such a strong hold on so many people's lives over such a long period of time largely because they are unforgettable.

Religious ideas, institutions, and professions are among the oldest in humanity's history. They have outlasted the world's great empires. Their authority and influence have endured far beyond that of Earth's greatest philosophers, military leaders, social engineers, or politicians. It is this that makes them so attractive to those who seek power and influence, whether such people intend to use their power and influence for good or evil. Unfortunately, in the hands of the wrong person, religious ideas might as easily be responsible for the destruction of the world as for its salvation. All that stands between us and that outcome is the knowledge of the general populace. In this as in any other field, people must be able to critically assess what they are being told.

The authors and editors of this series hope that all who seek to wield the tremendous powers of religion will do so with unselfish and noble intent. Knowing how unlikely it is that that will always be the case, we seek to provide the basic knowledge necessary to critically assess the degree to which contemporary religious claims are congruent with the history, scriptures, and genius of the traditions they are supposed to represent.

Ann Marie Bo Bahr
South Dakota State University

1

Introduction

We believe in one God,
The Father, the Almighty,
Maker of Heaven and earth,
Of all that is, seen and unseen.

—The Nicene Creed

As the world's largest and most widespread religion, Christianity has impacted the lives of both believers and nonbelievers. It has been a formative influence on the governments and legal codes of the most highly developed areas of the world. The fact that it is the dominant religion in the wealthy nations of the First World augments its global influence.

For two millennia, Christianity has been a factor, sometimes large and sometimes slight, in European science, art, literature, education, and philosophy. For the past several centuries, it has played the same role in both North and South America.

Today, Christianity continues to directly impact the thinking of one-third of the world on ethics, morals, marriage, parenting, and lifestyle issues. Needless to say, decisions in these areas influence all apsects of life. In addition, Christianity continues to shape our ideas of human nature, happiness, the just society, the meaning of life, and good and evil.

If we think of the world as a loaf of bread, we might think of Christianity not as the hands and mind that shaped the world from outside (Christians would say God does that), but as a leaven at work within it. The Christian yeast cells are not the only leaven in the dough, of course, nor are they evenly distributed, but one could find some of them just about anywhere one might choose to look. The bread of the world would have an entirely different shape and flavor if the Christian yeast had not been at work in it.

CHRIST: "YOU ARE THE CHRIST" (MARK 8:29)

"The Christ" is a title, not a proper name, just like "the Buddha." The name of the man Buddhists call "the Buddha" is Siddhartha Gautama of the Shakyas. The name of the man Christians call "Christ" is Jesus of Nazareth.

Christ is the Greek equivalent of the Hebrew word *messiah.* Both words mean "the anointed one."

In biblical times, certain people and objects were anointed— blessed with oil. In the Jerusalem Temple, the altar, its utensils, and the Ark of the Covenant (the sacred chest symbolizing God's relationship with the Jews) were anointed. Priests, prophets, and kings were among the people anointed. Anointing was a sign that someone was set aside for the service of God. Just as all Israel was a chosen people, a nation set apart for God, so, too, specific people within Israel were set apart for God.

When one was anointed, one's life was no longer his or her own. It belonged to God. The body of a person who had died was also anointed, indicating that the life of the person had been given back to God. Whether the rite was carried out when someone was dead or alive, anointing signified the handing over of one's life to God.

Jesus's first followers were Jews who were familiar with this concept of anointing. By calling Jesus "the Christ," they voiced their belief that his life was entirely dedicated to God, that God had chosen him for a special task. That task, Christians believe, was the salvation of the world. Hence, Jesus is also called "Savior" and "Redeemer."

When people become Christians today, they begin by learning who Jesus is. We must realize, however, that Jesus's first followers did not have anything like a complete idea of who he was until after he had died and risen. The first Christians reasoned *backward*, from what Jesus did to who he was. It was only *after* Jesus's life had run its full course that his followers realized what its purpose had been: His life was an offering for the redemption of the sins of humankind. It wasn't until after people saw what the one they had identified as the Messiah *did* that they were really able to understand what it meant to *be* the Messiah.

Being faithful Jews, they, of course, knew what the prophets of Israel had said about the coming of a Messiah. But prophecies weren't predictions, they were promises—promises that people knew they could trust because God, the faithful One of Israel, had made them.

The difference is this: In order to *predict* how something will turn out, you have to understand it very well. Your mind has to be capable of grasping it. No pious Jew could claim to know God's plans and purposes that well. They prayed to see the day of the Messiah's coming, without knowing exactly what would happen when the Messiah arrived. Any student of the Bible, in Jesus's time or in our own, runs the risk of thinking that he or she knows exactly what it means. Being wedded to their own preconceptions, people might miss what they are searching for.

Jesus healed people, preached about a God of amazing love and mercy, was crucified as a convicted criminal, and, according to the Gospel, rose again on the third day after his death. Acts of the Apostles records that Jesus was taken up into heaven forty days after his resurrection.

People were astounded by Jesus's words and deeds, but some questioned whether his power came from God or from Satan. Many of those who believed he was sent by God had to readjust their concept of God, for here was a God whose judgment involved passing out new life to believers rather than death sentences to sinners. Eventually, Christians would decide that no mere human being could have done what Jesus did.

CHRISTIANS

Christians are believers in, and followers of, Jesus. Christians agree about the central place of Jesus in God's plan for the salvation of the world, but they differ about many other things. The three main kinds of Christians are Orthodox, Catholics, and Protestants. Catholics and Protestants are often called Western Christians, while the Orthodox are Eastern Christians. Historically, Protestants have emphasized the salvation of the individual, Catholics the salvation of the world, and Orthodoxy the salvation of the entire cosmos, including the natural world.

Orthodox Christians

The Orthodox are organized into independent national churches. The two largest of these are the Greek Orthodox Church and the Russian Orthodox Church. The Orthodox have priests who may marry and monks who take a vow of celibacy. Bishops and those of higher rank are drawn from the monastic clergy. It is only priests who have the option to marry.

Monastic life has always been very important in Orthodoxy. It was the monasteries that kept the native religion and culture alive during times of foreign occupation. Monks do not belong to separate religious orders, as is the case among Roman Catholics.

Orthodox Christians once lived throughout the Middle East, but Islam is now the dominant religion in that part of the world. Today, the geographic center of Orthodox Christianity is Eastern Europe.

Orthodox churches are traditional. They place great importance on the continuity of the faith with its earliest forms. They practice a form of Christianity that was developed in the major cities of the Eastern Roman Empire during the first centuries A.D. The most important of these cities were Jerusalem (in present-day Israel), Alexandria (in present-day Egypt), and Antioch and Constantinople (in present-day Turkey).

In the Orthodox faith, there are seven sacraments: baptism, chrismation, eucharist, confession, marriage, priesthood, and anointing of the sick. Chrismation is anointing with oil. Among Western Christians it is called confirmation.

Orthodox theology emphasizes the Trinity. The doctrine of the Trinity states that there are three persons (Father, Son, and Holy Spirit) within the one God. Whereas some Christian churches tend to focus almost exclusively on Jesus, Orthodox Christianity pays equal attention to all three persons of the Trinity.

Another theological emphasis is the Incarnation. The Incarnation is the belief that God became human in Jesus. God actually took on flesh and blood, and lived a completely human life. Orthodox Christians believe that this imparts great dignity to the natural world, and to human beings in particular. One of the most frequently heard Orthodox phrases—"God became man so that man might become God"[1]—expresses this sense of the amazing possibilities opened up for humanity by the Incarnation.

Orthodox Christianity is famous for its worship services, which are several hours in length. They take place in richly decorated churches. The service is almost entirely sung or chanted, rather than spoken, but without musical accompaniment.

Orthodox Christianity is also known for its religious art. It developed a special kind of religious painting known as "icons." These are usually traditional religious images, such as portraits of saints, painted in rich colors on small wooden panels.

Catholic Christians

Catholicism is a single worldwide church under the leadership of the pope. Thanks to its centralized system of authority, it has no major subdivisions.[2] The administrative center of Catholicism is located at the Vatican in Rome.

The Catholic Church is served by priests, bishops, and cardinals, all of whom take a vow of celibacy. There are also monastic orders of monks and nuns (whose members also take a vow of chastity). These religious orders have names such as the Franciscans, the Benedictines, and the Jesuits.

Prior to the sixteenth century, all of Western Europe was united in a single Christian Church. After the Reformation (which began in 1517), Catholic strength centered in southern Europe. Today, the continents with the largest number of Catholics are South America and Africa. In the United States, about one-quarter of the population is Catholic. Mexico is predominantly Catholic, as is the Canadian province of Quebec.

The Catholic Church has the same seven sacraments as Orthodox churches, though some are called by different names. For Catholics (and for the Orthodox), a sacrament is more than a remembrance. It is believed to impart the presence, merits, and grace of Jesus Christ to the recipient. It actually effects a change in the person who receives it.

Catholic theology has an analogical style, which means that it tends to see differences as complementary rather than antagonistic. Protestant theology, on the other hand, is dialectical, which means it works through opposition. For example, Protestants tend to oppose faith and reason, while Catholics combine them. Protestants usually see the Bible and tradition in opposition, whereas Catholics view them as mutually supportive.

Whereas Protestants look to the Bible alone as the source of religious truth, Catholics use tradition to help them understand the Bible. As Protestants see it, tradition is dangerous because it may add to or subtract from God's word as found in the Bible. Some Protestants avoid relying on tradition altogether, while others retain it while making sure that it is kept strictly subservient to the Bible.

Catholics do not think the Bible opposes tradition. Rather, the Bible itself is seen as a product of early Christian tradition. In addition to the Bible, which is first in importance, the other components of Catholic tradition are the teachings of the early Church Fathers, the twenty-one ecumenical councils of the Church (meetings at which ideas are exchanged and debated), and the encyclicals (universal letters) issued by the popes.

Catholics are known for their veneration of Mary, the mother of Jesus, and other very holy people called "saints." Like the Orthodox, but unlike Protestants, they may even pray to these deceased people. Protestants consider this practice to be flirting with idolatry, but Catholic and Orthodox Christians believe that the saints can and do pray to God for living believers, and that their prayers are very powerful because they are in heaven.

Protestant Christians
There are many subdivisions of Protestantism. Lutherans, Reformed Churches, Methodists, and Baptists are just a few of the many types of Protestant Christianity. These subdivisions of Protestantism are usually called denominations.

The organizational structure of the different denominations varies. Some denominations (e.g., Methodists and Lutherans) have bishops. Others have regional and national governing boards, but no bishops (e.g., Presbyterians). Still others acknowledge no authority beyond the local congregation (e.g., Baptists).

Protestant churches are led by ministers rather than priests. Ministers are usually permitted to marry. Protestant churches do not have monks or nuns. Anglicans (Episcopalians) are the sole exception—they have priests and a few small monastic orders. Anglican priests, however, may marry, and they may be either male or female.

Protestantism is the dominant form of Christianity in the northern sections of Western Europe, the United States, Canada, and other countries that were once British colonies. Because many First World nations are predominantly Protestant, this form of Christianity enjoys an influence beyond its numbers.

The Anglican, or Episcopalian, Church is the only Protestant denomination to retain all seven sacraments. Many Protestant churches have two sacraments: baptism and the Lord's Supper. Others have no sacraments at all. However, Protestants may still be baptized, take communion, and be confirmed even if they do not consider these rituals sacraments. They simply do not invest these actions with the sacramental power that Orthodox and Catholic Christians attribute to them.

Protestant theology emphasizes justification by grace alone, or through faith alone. In other words, Protestants stress that our salvation is a completely free and unmerited gift from God. There is nothing that human beings can do to gain salvation. This outlook results in a greater emphasis on the work of Jesus than is given by other Christians. Protestants tend to magnify the name of Jesus beyond that of the other two persons of the Trinity.

Protestants insisted that worship services and the Bible should be in the language of the people. They emphasize the importance of reading and studying the Bible. They have also been the musical innovators of the Christian world.

Anglicans

Although they comprise only about 5 percent of U.S. Protestants, Anglicans constitute one of the largest Christian bodies worldwide. As the official church of England, Anglicanism spread along with the British Empire. It now has an active presence in more than 160 countries. In the United States, Anglicans are called Episcopalians.

The Anglican Church has one foot in the Protestant camp, and the other with the Catholics. It has the same seven sacraments as Catholics do. It honors the saints and celebrates their feast days. It has priests rather than ministers, but unlike the Catholic clergy, its priests are allowed to marry. Women as well as men may become priests.

Anglicans tolerate theological differences of opinion. They believe in "unity in essentials and liberty in nonessentials."[3] The unifying factor among Anglicans is the use of the Book of Common Prayer, a special service book first issued in 1549, in public worship.

The Church of England has always valued intellectual life; its theologians regularly dialogue with secular fields of study. In fact, the Episcopal Church requires its clergy to hold university as well as seminary degrees. Physicist Isaac Newton (1642–1727) is but one example of a famous scientist who was also an Anglican clergyman and theologian. Perhaps the best-known Anglican literary figure is C. S. Lewis.

Lutherans

The Lutheran Church is named after Martin Luther (1483–1546), who is usually regarded as the founder of the Protestant Reformation. Luther taught that we are saved by grace alone, and that only faith in God is necessary for salvation. This concept implies that churches, priests to administer the sacraments, and good works are *not* necessary for salvation.

Lutherans believe that the Bible is the sole rule of faith. Creeds and tradition are valued, but their importance is secondary to that of the Bible itself.

Luther insisted on the separation of law and Gospel. Lutherans are taught to obey the law and support legitimate political authority, but they do not mix secular and religious authority. Consequently, Lutherans have never attempted to establish theocratic states—that is, countries in which biblical law also serves as the political law of the nation.

Lutherans are famous for their hymns and for their charity.

Lutheran Services in America takes in more donated money than any other charitable agency in the United States, almost twice as much as its nearest competitor. Of the $7.6 billion that Lutheran Services in America collected for charity in 2002, only around $500 million was spent on administration.

There are many Lutherans in Germany, where Martin Luther lived. The Lutheran Church is the state church in Denmark, Norway, Sweden, and Finland.

Reformed Churches

The Reformed Churches include the Congregational, Presbyterian, United, and Reformed churches. These institutions subscribe to a Calvinist theology, which means that they trace their roots back to sixteenth-century French reformer John Calvin (1509–1564). By education, Calvin was a lawyer and a humanist (one who has studied the subjects now included in the humanities, such as languages, literature, and speech).

The writing styles of Luther and Calvin make an interesting study in contrasts. Luther was passionate and colorful. Calvin was orderly and systematic. Following Calvin, Reformed ministers are trained in orderly, systematic thought.

Reformed theology emphasizes God's sovereignty and the utter inability of human beings to accomplish their own salvation. This may seem to be a recipe for laziness, but it is not. The Reformed Churches foster hard work and frugality, since these are taken to be signs that a person is among the "elect"—that he or she has been chosen by God to share in eternal life. Calvinist Christians believe that humanity's purpose is to glorify and enjoy God forever.

Calvinist churches teach that God's grace is irresistible, that it cannot be rejected by any individual to whom God offers it. One Reformed minister explained irresistible grace to me in this way: "It's like being really thirsty, and having to decide whether to accept a bottle of water or not. Is that really a choice?"[4] On the other hand, one to whom grace has not been given can do nothing to attain it. This doctrine is called "predestination."

Calvin established theocratic rule in Geneva. The Puritans, who established theocratic colonies in what is now New England, were Calvin's theological heirs in this regard.

Methodists

Methodism began in the eighteenth century with the preaching of John Wesley. Methodism is a descendant of the Anglican Church.

Probably the most distinctive aspect of Methodist theology is its emphasis on God's universal offer of salvation, and on the reality and significance of human free will in accepting or rejecting it. This belief is called Arminianism, after Jacobus Arminius, a Dutch theologian who opposed the Calvinist doctrines of predestination and irresistible grace.

Methodists are known for their active involvement in social issues and causes, combined with an emphasis on personal holiness. Along with Lutherans and Baptists, they are also renowned for their love of singing. Charles Wesley, John's brother, was one of Christianity's most famous hymn writers.

Methodist ministers may be either women or men. They go to serve congregations where they are sent by their bishop. They are itinerate, meaning that they move around. In the nineteenth century, Methodist clergy rode on horseback from one congregation to the next. They were called "circuit riders."

The Methodists are the third-largest religious body in the United States, right after Catholics and Baptists.

Baptists

"There are no Baptists by birth, only by rebirth," said a prominent poster in one Baptist church I visited. This statement points to several distinguishing features of Baptists. First, they do not baptize infants. Baptism is reserved for people who are old enough to understand what they are doing when they make a personal commitment to Jesus Christ. The second Baptist characteristic suggested by the statement is the importance of being "born again." To be "born again" means to realize that one is a sinner who needs the salvation offered by Jesus, and to choose to turn one's life over to Christ.

Baptist congregations are self-governing (autonomous); they do not believe they need to obey any human authority beyond the local level in religious matters. Because Baptists were often persecuted in the seventeenth century, they became strong defenders of religious freedom and proponents of the separation of church and state.

Baptists are committed to missionary efforts; their missionaries have spread the Baptist form of Christianity to all the continents. However, Baptists are most strongly represented in the United States, where they are the largest Protestant denomination.

Evangelicals and Pentecostals

Evangelicalism and Pentecostalism are not Protestant denominations. Rather, they are religious movements that attract participants from many different denominations. In their contemporary form, both of these movements began in the United States. Evangelicals are the descendants of the First and Second Great Awakening (of the 1730s–1770s and 1790s–1840s, respectively), and of the revivals of the first half of the nineteenth century. Pentecostals are descendants of the Holiness Movement in nineteenth-century America, which, in turn, was a development of John Wesley's notion of sanctification.

Like the United States itself, these movements are characterized by an emphasis on the individual as opposed to the communal. They value personal religious experience, demand an individual choice for Jesus, and stress individual versus social responsibility for wrongdoing.

Just as the Anglican Church gained a worldwide following through its association with British expansion in the nineteenth century, so evangelicals and Pentecostals are showing global gains through their association with American wealth and world leadership.

Evangelicals. It is more difficult to define an evangelical than it is to define a Lutheran or a Methodist, because evangelicals belong to a popular movement that may span several denominations rather than being one organization. Most evangelicals share the following characteristics: They are committed to the inerrancy of the Bible; they believe in the inborn sinfulness of human beings; they subscribe to the necessity of a "born again" experience, as well as the need for a personal relationship with Jesus Christ; and they emphasize the importance of Matthew 28:19 ("Go therefore and make disciples of all nations . . ."), which they call the "Great Commission."

Evangelicals believe that every Christian should be engaged in some form of missionary work. This sense of mission, when combined with American wealth, competitive spirit, and political power, has unfortunately led in recent years to a kind of Christian "empire building." Some American evangelicals are claiming for Christianity precisely the kinds of world leadership that Jesus himself took great pains to avoid (John 6:15), and to teach his disciples to avoid (Mark 9:33–37, 10:21–25, 10:41–45).

Traditionally, evangelicalism has been a reform and renewal movement. Indeed, its refusal to engage in Christian political agendas is what once differentiated it from fundamentalism. This split between evangelicals and fundamentalists (which appears to be diminishing) was the result of decisions made by Billy Graham.

Graham (b. 1918) was the leading evangelical of the twentieth century. It was his fame that put the movement on the map. He became the all-American evangelist by transcending doctrine and denomination. In 1956, he founded *Christianity Today* magazine, a popular religious journal that has attempted to maintain Graham's vision of the evangelical movement.

Graham avoided the political agenda of the Christian Right, and drew criticism from his more narrow-minded colleagues for his willingness to cooperate with mainstream and liberal Protestants. Bob Jones (the founder of Bob Jones University) accused Graham of peddling a "discount type of religion" and "sacrificing the cause of evangelism on the altar of temporary convenience."[5] Graham countered, "Christians are not limited to any church. The only question is: are you committed to Christ?"[6] While Bob Jones became a fundamentalist leader, Billy Graham made evangelicalism a global movement on a par with the Roman Catholic Church and the World Council of Churches.

Pentecostals. The fastest-growing Christian movement, both worldwide and in the United States, is the Pentecostal movement. If current expansion rates continue, it could challenge the Catholic Church for status as the largest type of Christianity in the world in just another twenty-five years or so.

Pentecostals emphasize baptism in the Holy Spirit and the manifestation of the gifts of the Spirit in the lives of believers. They believe that people can receive the Holy Spirit today in the same way that the Bible says the Apostles did on the day of Pentecost. On that day, according to Acts of the Apostles, there was a powerful wind, and tongues of fire came to rest on the head of each of the Apostles (2:1–3).

The reception of certain gifts accompanies the baptism in the Holy Spirit. One such gift is the ability to talk in a language not known by the speaker. This is called "speaking in tongues." Other gifts include healing, prophecy, the interpretation of tongues, wisdom, and knowledge.

The largest Pentecostal denomination is the Assemblies of God, which has a worldwide membership of 32 million. I spoke with an Assemblies of God minister, a former air force master sergeant. His vision of the church is that it should be a gathering directed by the Holy Spirit and the power of God, not dominated by human reason or influence.

Although Pastor Dan Campbell doesn't view the Pentecostal experience as a requirement to go to heaven, he cannot understand why any Christian would not want to "get filled up with and given over to the power of God." The baptism of the Holy Spirit, he said, is "a second work of grace."[7]

THE GROWTH OF CHRISTIANITY

The ancient Roman system of roads was so well built that sections of it still exist today. Using these roads, Jesus's followers began to spread the message of his life, death, and resurrection. By A.D. 60, local churches had been established in most of the major cities of the Roman Empire.

Although Christians faced intermittent persecution for the first three centuries, Christianity continued to grow. Around A.D. 300, Armenia (a former Western Asian kingdom, southwest of the Caspian Sea) became the first nation to officially declare itself Christian.

By the beginning of the fourth century, Christians were tolerated and permitted to practice their religion in the Roman Empire. By the end of that century, Christianity had become the official religion of the empire.

Beginning around 450, Nestorian Christians evangelized in the Persian Empire. Nestorian Christians are neither Orthodox nor Catholic. They differ from other Christians in their belief that Jesus had two separate natures—one human and one divine—rather than one nature that combined both elements. Although they make up a very tiny sect of Christianity today, Nestorians managed to plant their faith in Iran, Iraq, China, India, and Afghanistan. Baghdad was the main center of the Nestorian Church for most of its history. However, due to the recent turmoil in Iraq, the leader of the Nestorian Church now lives in another country.

By the fifth century, most of the Middle East and North Africa was Christian. However, after Islam appeared in the seventh century and began its expansion outward from its heartland in Saudi Arabia, all of this territory gradually came under Muslim control. Christian growth was effectively halted in these areas, because Muslims are not allowed to convert to another religion. Today, this part of the world has only small Christian communities.

In the meantime, Christianity was spreading north from the Mediterranean area. By the late thirteenth century, all of Europe, including Russia, was Christian. European peoples living as far north as Scandinavia and as far east as Poland and Hungary were converted to the Western form of Christianity, centered in Rome. Their type of Christianity would eventually become the Roman Catholic Church. The Bulgarians, Ukrainians, Serbs, and Russians, however, owed their style of worship to Constantinople rather than Rome. Their form of worship would be eventually be known as Orthodox Christianity.

The worldwide expansion of Christianity, which has been continuously progressing for the past five centuries, began in Europe. It was the result of Catholic and Protestant missionary activity. The missionaries traveled with the colonialists. European colonialism was a process by which large segments of the globe were brought under the political and economic control of one or another of the European nations. The European nations were, in effect, vying for control of non-European territory to help enrich and empower themselves.

The Spanish and Portuguese created the first colonial empires. Beginning in the sixteenth century, they gained control of South America, Central America, and the southern portion of North America. The missionaries who accompanied the colonizers were Catholic, and that part of the world remains predominantly Catholic to this day.

French Catholic missionaries traveled with the explorers of territory that eventually became part of what is now Canada and the United States. Canada remains close to 50 percent Catholic, with the province of Quebec being mainly Catholic. It was British Protestant missionaries who made the largest imprint on the rest of Canada and on the United States. Today, the United States is home to more Protestants than any other country in the world.

Beginning in the nineteenth century, scores of Christian missionaries (most of them Anglican, Reformed, or Catholic) traveled to sub-Saharan Africa. By 2000, there were more than 150 million Christians in Africa, out of a total population of nearly 800 million. The division between those of Catholic and Protestant persuasion is fairly even.

COUNTING CHRISTIANS

Religious statistics should always be viewed as approximations. First, not all countries keep track of religious affiliation (the United States, for example, does not). Second, religions have no standardized way to count members. Some religions allow dual affiliation (e.g., a Buddhist may also practice Shinto in Japan) and others (e.g., Judaism, Christianity, and Islam) do not. Even among Christians, there is no one way of counting members. Some churches count only mature, professing adults, while others count baptized infants. That said, it is still interesting to compare reported membership numbers.

Included in this chart are both organizations (such as the World Methodist Council or the Catholic Church) and movements that cut across organizational lines (such as Pentecostalism and evangelicalism). Therefore, it is possible for one person to be counted twice—a person might be counted as a member of both the World Evangelical Alliance and the Baptist World Alliance.

LARGEST CHRISTIAN GROUPS WORLDWIDE

GROUP	WORLD ADHERENTS
1) Catholic Church	1 billion 50 million
2) Pentecostals	500 million
3) Orthodox Church	225 million
4) World Evangelical Alliance	200 million
5) Anglican Communion	76 million
6) World Alliance of Reformed Churches	75 million (Congregational, Presbyterian Reformed, and United)
7) World Methodist Council	36 million, with a wider community of 70 million
8) Lutheran World Federation	64 million
9) Baptist World Alliance	44 million

The most recent wave of Christian expansion began in the nineteenth century, strengthened in the twentieth century, and continues today. This time, the Christian missionaries are most often American evangelicals and Pentecostals. They are bringing their conservative form of Protestant Christianity to all parts of the globe. They have been most successful in Asia, Latin America, and sub-Saharan Africa.

By 1750, Christianity was more widespread than any religion had ever been before, and it retains that distinction today. Christianity is also the largest religion in the world, with nearly 2 billion people, approximately one-third of the global population, in its fold.

2

Jesus of Nazareth

*The result was that when Jesus had finished
these words [the Sermon on the Mount],
the multitudes were amazed at His teaching;
for He was teaching them as one having authority . . .*

—Matthew 7:28–29

ROMAN OCCUPATION

Jesus was born when Rome ruled the world. At the time of his birth, the Roman Empire included all the areas bordering the Mediterranean Sea, plus all of Western Europe except the British Isles, Scandinavia, and Germany. Judaea (part of ancient Palestine) was a tributary when Jesus was born. It was annexed in A.D. 6. Although Rome boasted military, political, and economic dominance, the culture of the Roman Empire was still Greek.

Rome had been a republic until just a few decades before the birth of Jesus. The republican system changed during the reigns of Julius Caesar (who lived 100–44 B.C.) and his nephew Augustus (63 B.C.–A.D. 14), however. Beguiled by expansion and besieged by war, Rome consolidated authority in one man, the emperor. In its attempt to control a vast territory, the Roman Empire not only stripped conquered peoples of their freedom, but it also divested its own citizens of the republican form of government. It did have good points, though.

It was one of the proud claims of the empire that it brought "peace to Rome and quiet to the provinces."[8] It established an enviable system of roads, along which Christian missionaries would carry the message of Jesus. The empire also brought law and order. The Roman system of law became a source for most modern European law codes, and also for canon law ("Church law," which is still used by the Catholic Church today).

No doubt the Romans thought they were improving the lives of the conquered peoples, whom they called "barbarians" (which literally meant "foreigners," but carried the connotation that the conquered people were uncivilized). Not all the conquered peoples were happy, however. Many Jews had deep reservations about the Roman occupation, if not outright hatred of it. The Jews believed their God had called them to be a special nation, set apart from others. They were to separate themselves from the evils of the rest of the world and live according to the law of their God. As part of the Roman Empire, Israel could not be a nation apart. It was part of the Roman system. Its own religious leaders had to collaborate with Rome as the price for national survival. And

Israel could not avoid learning and following at least some of the ways of the Gentile (non-Jewish) nations. Roman soldiers and administrators were everywhere. In the eyes of pious Jews, they polluted the land.

We know of four different kinds of Jewish response to Roman rule. Jesus of Nazareth was not associated with any of them. However, we can better understand the uniqueness of Jesus if we know something about the options he did *not* take.

The Sadducees

The Sadducees were wealthy conservatives associated with the Jerusalem Temple. This priestly aristocracy sat at the top of Palestine's social pyramid, from which vantage point they ran Jewish domestic affairs. They were the ruling elite. They were not very popular with the common people.

The Sadducees accepted only what was written in the Bible as authoritative. One of the contested issues of Jesus's time was whether or not there would be a resurrection of the dead. The Sadducees rejected the notion of resurrection, because there was no reference to it in the Law or the Prophets, the two parts of the Bible that had been canonized by the time of Jesus.

To the best of our knowledge, Jesus was not wealthy. He believed that there would be a resurrection. He was far more popular with the common people than he was with the ruling elite. Jesus was not a Sadducee.

The Pharisees

The Pharisees were popular with the people. Professionally, they were artisans, shopkeepers, or landowners. They were also scholars and teachers of the Law. While they were not usually among the poorest of Jews, they were not among the wealthiest either.

The Pharisees were interested in being observant Jews—that is, in living according to the Torah (narrowly, the first five books of the Bible, but broadly the entire Jewish Bible, which is the same set of books as the Christian Old Testament). Unlike the Sadducees, they did not limit God's revelation to what was written. They developed and expanded Mosaic Law (Jewish law, from the institutions or writings related to Moses) as they applied it to the new questions and concerns that arose as a result of living in an ever-changing world.

The Sabbath laws provide an example of how this worked. The Bible clearly prohibits work on the Sabbath, but it nowhere specifically states what should be considered work. The Pharisees undertook the task of spelling out exactly what would be forbidden on the Sabbath. Such interpretations and expansions of Torah went beyond what was written in the Bible, but they were necessary to apply biblical teaching to everyday life. They were known as Oral Torah. It was Oral Torah that the Sadducees rejected.

Although Jesus agreed with the Pharisees on several key issues, such as the reality of the resurrection, he was not a Pharisee. He knew the Bible well and could use it to his advantage in an argument, but this was not Jesus's preferred method of teaching. He never argued about the meaning or application of Scripture unless he was challenged by someone. He preferred to make lessons out of his observations of ordinary life: shepherds and sheep, women baking bread, rain falling on the just and unjust, farmers sowing seeds.

Jesus's lack of Pharisaic meticulousness about the Law showed up in his willingness to heal on the Sabbath (Matthew 12:9–14) and to allow his disciples to pick grain on the Sabbath (Matthew 12:1–8). He also apparently ignored the purity laws on more than one occasion, for example, by eating with Gentiles and sinners, or by allowing a woman who was hemorrhaging to touch him. (The purity laws called for Jews to observe strict separation from Gentiles, sinners, or anything that might render them impure. Any kind of bodily discharge, such as blood, was considered polluting.)

Zealots

Like the Pharisees, the Zealots were strictly observant Jews who believed that the Gentiles polluted the land. Unlike the Pharisees, though, they believed that faithfulness to Israel's God demanded the overthrow of the Roman government. Recognizing the Roman emperor as lord, or using coins imprinted with his image, appeared to the Zealots to be violations of the First Commandment, which ordered that people should have no gods or representations of gods other than the one true God (Exodus 20:2–3).

Though one of Jesus's disciples may have been a Zealot (see Luke 6:15 and Acts 1:13), Jesus himself was not. When asked whether it were right to pay taxes, he replied that one should "render unto to Caesar what is Caesar's, and unto God what belongs to God" (Mark 12:17). This implied that it was possible to live under Roman rule and still do what God requires. In addition, Jesus seems to have had few kind words for armed resistance. With one possible exception (Luke 22:35–38), he consistently advises against combating evil with worldly forms of power.

Essenes

The Essenes, like the Zealots, believed that the Gentiles polluted the land. In their opinion, even the Jerusalem Temple was contaminated, because it was served by corrupt priests who had been appointed by Gentile kings. Unlike the Zealots, however, the Essenes did not advocate armed resistance to remove the foreign influence. Rather than driving out the polluters, they chose to move away from the pollution.

The Essenes separated themselves from society and lived in communes. Here, they followed a strict discipline and kept company only with each other, believing even fellow Jews to be unclean. In addition to trying to live according to the Scriptures, they dedicated themselves to making copies of various biblical scrolls. One of these communities produced the Dead Sea Scrolls discovered near Qumran, in the West Bank near the shore of the Dead Sea, in 1947.

Jesus did not advocate separating oneself from the impure. He was notorious for his habit of talking to known sinners and even eating at their tables. Jesus appears not to have been married but, other than that, he did not live a monastic lifestyle.

JESUS'S LIFE

The New Testament records that Jesus was born to a woman named Mary, who was engaged to marry a man named Joseph (Matthew 1:18, Luke 1:27). It states that at the time of the conception, Mary was a virgin. Jesus is said to have been conceived by the power of the Holy Spirit (Luke 1:35).

Between Jesus's birth and his public life as an adult, the New Testament records only a few incidents. The Gospels focus on Jesus's public life, a period of between one and three years, when Jesus was in his early thirties.

DATES OF JESUS'S BIRTH AND DEATH

We do not know exactly when Jesus of Nazareth was born, or exactly when he died. Only the birth and death dates of the most prominent people were recorded in Roman Palestine.

We know that Jesus was born during the time of Emperor Augustus, who reigned from 27 B.C. to A.D. 14. Matthew's Gospel tells us that Jesus was born when Herod was king of Judaea. Assuming that Matthew meant Herod the Great (not Herod Antipas), Jesus must have been born in or prior to 4 B.C., because Herod died in that year. However, we do not know in which year of Herod's reign Jesus was born. Matthew's Gospel simply says, "In the time of King Herod . . ." (2:1).

Matthew also tells us that Herod ordered all the children of Bethlehem who were two years old or under killed, "according to the time that he had learned from the wise men" (2:16). It would be helpful if there were a Roman record of this event, but none has been found. The implication of Matthew's statement is that Jesus may have been born two years prior to the slaughter of the Bethlehem children—that is, in 6 B.C. or earlier. We do not know how long after that event Herod died.

All four Gospels record that Jesus died when Pontius Pilate was governor of Judaea—that is, between A.D. 26 and 36. Matthew, Mark, and Luke state that Jesus died on Passover day, and that the next day was the Sabbath. This was the case in A.D. 27. John, however, states that Jesus died on the day before Passover, and that the next day was both Passover and the Sabbath. This would have been true in A.D. 30 and again in 33. If Jesus was born between 4 and 6 B.C., he would have been between thirty-one and thirty-nine years old when he was crucified.

Jesus was a healer. Among the infirmities he is said to have healed are leprosy, paralysis, blindness, fever, deafness, deformed back, and demon possession. Healing through nonmedical techniques was not unusual in Jesus's day. Except for the very wealthy, most people who sought help for a sickness would look to people we would call faith healers today. There were physicians available, but often only the rich could afford them.

Apparently, Jesus healed so many people that he found it difficult to escape the crowds who pressed upon him, begging for attention to their needs. He gained the admiration of the people in this way (Mark 7:37), but no first-century Jew would have concluded that he was divine because of his healings. Instead, they would have seen Jesus's healings as evidence of the power of God's spirit flowing through him (see Matthew 12:28, Mark 5:30). In the Hebrew Scriptures, such spirit-filled people had been used as prophets and helpers of those in need. Elijah, for example, was a prophet who brought a widow's dead son back to life (1 Kings 17:17–24). Perhaps this is why some people thought Jesus was Elijah returned (Matthew 16:14).

However unusual Jesus's healing abilities might have been, his teaching talent appears to have been even more astounding. The Gospel writer Luke records that, at twelve years of age, Jesus sat in the midst of the teachers of Israel and engaged in a conversation with them at their own scholarly level. Whether or not this story is historical, it shows Jesus's reputation for very unusual wisdom. In Jesus's hometown of Nazareth, those who heard him speak in the synagogue were "astonished by the gracious words that came from his lips" (Luke 4:22). Those who heard Jesus teach in the Temple in Jerusalem had a similar reaction (Luke 7:15); one group even proclaimed, "No one has ever spoken like this man!" (Luke 7:46).

Jesus's teaching took the form of wisdom sayings and parables. An example of the former, a wisdom saying, is: "No one can serve two masters; for a slave will either hate the one and love the other, or be devoted to the one and despise the other. You cannot serve God and wealth" (Matthew 6:24). An example of the latter is the well-known parable of the prodigal son (Luke 15:11–32).

THE PARABLE OF THE PRODIGAL SON

Jesus's famous parable about the "prodigal son" can be found in the Gospel of Luke. According to the story, a man had two sons. One day, the younger of the two demanded, "Father, give me my share of the estate." So the man divided his property between his two sons. Soon after receiving his inheritance, the younger son took all of his belongings and left for a distant country, where he spent all his money living a life of luxury and excess.

Eventually, he lost all of his inheritance. At the same time, a terrible famine hit the country, and he found himself in danger of starvation. At first, he signed on as a laborer in the fields of a local citizen, but he was overcome with hunger for the food he had to feed to the animals, and couldn't convince anyone to give him any food. Finally, the thought occurred to him that he should simply return home to his father, explain that he is starving, and ask for forgiveness.

Before he even reached home, his father met up with him and was filled with love and compassion for his lost son. He ran to the son and embraced him. The son said, "Father, I have sinned against heaven and against you. I am no longer worthy to be called your son." Dismissing these words, the father said to his servants, "Quick! Bring the best robe and put it on him. Put a ring on his finger and sandals on his feet. Bring the fattened calf and kill it. Let's have a feast and celebrate. For this son of mine was dead and is alive again; he was lost and is found." So they began to celebrate.

While all this was going on, the father's other son, who had remained at home when the younger son left, was at work in the fields. As he approached the house, he could hear the sounds of music and dancing inside. When he asked what was happening, one of the servants told him that his younger brother had returned and that "your father has killed the fattened calf because he has him back safe and sound."

The older brother grew angry and would not go into the house. He complained to his father, "All these years I've been slaving for you and never disobeyed your orders. Yet you never gave me even a young goat so I could celebrate with my friends. But when this son of yours who has squandered your property with prostitutes comes home, you kill the fattened calf for him!"

"My son," the father replied, "you are always with me, and everything I have is yours. But we had to celebrate and be glad, because this brother of yours was dead and is alive again; he was lost and is found."

Source: Luke 15:11–32

Wisdom sayings and parables differ markedly from scientific and technical language. The goal of the latter is precision and objectivity. The aim of Jesus's speech, on the other hand, was to get people to see the truth, and then live it. This required intuitive, imaginative insight far more than it required objective precision. For that reason, Jesus's teaching was evocative, provocative, and invitational. Jesus's parables of the Kingdom of Heaven *evoked* an imaginative assessment of what the Kingdom of God on Earth might be like. He challenged people to examine their assumptions about what God was like, or about justice. This is *provocative* language. He *invited* people to step into the world described in his stories and speeches. Whoever followed him there found an open door to the Kingdom of Heaven.

Teachers function in society in one of two ways: They can teach people how to live successfully in the world created by society, or they can challenge the assumptions held by that society. The first method of teaching is called conventional wisdom; it is the socialization process. The second is called alternative wisdom; it encourages independent, critical thinking. Jesus was a practitioner of alternative wisdom. At every turn, he challenged the assumptions of the religious custodians of his world.

Conventional wisdom taught Law-abiding people to avoid sinners and tax collectors; Jesus kept company with such folk. Conventional wisdom saw God as a distant, demanding lawgiver and judge; Jesus thought of God as someone who answered every need (Matthew 6:32), for the unrighteous as well as the righteous (Matthew 5:45). Every self-respecting Jew of Jesus's time avoided Samaritans, since they were considered obnoxious heretics (they did not worship at the Jerusalem Temple, but instead at Mount Gerizim, and they even had their own version of the Torah). Yet Jesus traveled through Samaritan territory (many Jews refused to do so) and spoke with the people (John 4). He even told a now-famous story in which a Samaritan was the hero (Luke 10:30–37)! Though Jesus did not agree with Samaritan religious beliefs (see John 4:22), he knew true righteousness when he saw it.

The words of Jesus were challenging. They made people think hard about God, their neighbors, and righteousness. The actions of Jesus were equally challenging—not necessarily his miracles, but his everyday actions, which defied the social structure established by purity concerns.

Because of the Roman occupation, Jews of Jesus's day could not use the political structure to enforce God's Law. They could, however, attempt to order society according to the Scriptures. They did this by imposing a biblically based set of purity laws on first-century Palestine. Purity laws generated the central social structure of Jesus's world.

A purity system divides the world up into two basic categories: pure and impure, or clean and unclean. The goal is to keep the impure from contaminating the pure. Since sinners and Gentiles were considered impure, good Jews were supposed to avoid them. Males and females were to be kept separate, for women were considered to be less pure than men. A woman was especially impure during her menstrual period, after childbirth, or whenever she had any flow of blood. She was to avoid going out in public at such times, lest she come into contact with a man and rob him of his strength by rendering him impure. The poor and diseased were viewed as impure, while the rich and healthy were pure. Even among Jewish men, there were different degrees of purity. A priest had to maintain a greater degree of purity than an ordinary man. The high priest had to have the greatest degree of purity.

The Jerusalem Temple was the center of control for the purity system. A person went there to be purified from sin or any other impurity. The Temple reflected purity divisions in its very structure: Only the high priest could enter the Holy of Holies (the innermost chamber of the Temple), and even he did so only once a year. There were separate courts for the priests, Jewish men, and Jewish women; each of these was progressively farther away from the Holy of Holies, since each marked a decrease in purity. The outermost court was reserved for the Gentiles, the most impure of all.

When Jesus challenged the purity laws (see, e.g., Mark 7:1–23), he was challenging the very structure of first-century Jewish society. When he forgave sins without recourse to the Temple or its system of purification (Mark 2:1–23), he undercut the system of religious authority that had the power to pronounce some people clean and others unclean. When he "cleansed the Temple," he implied that the place where purification was bestowed was itself unclean. Jesus was not a political revolutionary like the Zealots, but actions like his were certainly socially revolutionary.

Jesus was a social revolutionary in other ways, too. He touched those whom the purity system isolated as unclean (e.g., lepers or sinners), and he allowed them to touch him (e.g., the woman with the hemorrhage). In first-century Palestine, such people were literally "untouchables." Jesus also defied social law in regard to the treatment of women. Jesus not only spoke with women, but visited their homes and defended their right to be out in public following him as his disciples and contributing resources to his ministry.

Some of the religious authorities, it appears, were not pleased with Jesus's challenge to the purity system and to their own authority. It was they who plotted Jesus's death.

JESUS'S DEATH
The hardest thing to understand about the life of Jesus is the way it ended. People expected the Messiah to overthrow evil, not to be crucified by its henchmen.

Even Jesus's closest disciples rejected the idea of a suffering Messiah. In the Gospel of Mark, Jesus tells his disciples three times that he will have to suffer and die (8:31, 9:31, and 10:32–34). They do not understand what Jesus is trying to tell them. Peter, their spokesperson, even rebukes Jesus for saying such a thing (Mark 8:32).

When Jesus is finally crucified, the immediate reaction of his followers is one of fear (Mark 16:8), grief (John 20:11), and numb incomprehension (Luke 24:13–31). Even the joy of seeing Jesus risen from the dead was not enough to bring full understanding. Right before he ascended into heaven, his disciples were still waiting for Jesus to do the things that they thought the Messiah was supposed to do: drive out the Romans and reign from the throne of the restored Kingdom of Israel (Acts 1:6).

It was only over time that the young Christian community began to articulate the meaning of Jesus's death. Each evangelist explained the suffering and death of the Messiah in his own way.

Mark

Mark argued that Jesus's suffering and death, far from proving that he was not the Messiah, actually proved that he *was* the Messiah. When James and John, two of the Apostles, jostled for prime places in the Kingdom of God, Jesus took the opportunity to teach his followers that a true king would seek not to be served but to serve. A true king, Jesus said, would not lord it over his people, but would willingly give his life to save them. A true king is one who suffers in his followers' stead, rather than making them suffer for him (Mark 10:42–45). Mark concluded that Jesus's life and death proved that he was the Messiah, the true king of Israel.

Matthew

In Matthew's Gospel, Jesus is the supremely obedient one. Three times in the garden of Gethsemane in Jerusalem, he prays for God's will to be done, even if it be contrary to Jesus's own will (Matthew 26:39, 42, 44). Jesus's death is a deliberate fulfillment of God the Father's will as recorded in the Scriptures (Matthew 26:53–54).

Jesus is taunted and mocked as he hangs on the cross. His harassers tell him to come down from the cross and save himself if he truly is the son of God, if he truly is the king of Israel. Although, according to Christian belief, Jesus had the power to do so, he did not precisely because he *was* the true son of God and the true king of Israel—that is, he remained above all obedient to God's will. It was his father's will that he should die.

It is the job of the king, the son of God, to carry out God's commands. Jesus did so.

Luke

Luke shows Jesus at prayer far more often than any of the other evangelists do. This prayerful relationship with God the Father is not disrupted by the crucifixion. Jesus continues to address God, even from the cross, in a spirit of trust and faith. He prays for forgiveness for those who are torturing him (Luke 23:34). He voices his assurance that he will shortly be in paradise (Luke 23:43). Finally, at the moment of death, he places his spirit in his father's hands (Luke 23:46).

Jesus's close relationship with God the Father enables him to see both the necessity of his suffering (Luke 24:26), and the fact that it was part of God's plan (Luke 24:27). The crucifixion is neither a tragedy nor a catastrophe. Through it, God acts to save the world. Jesus, for his part, fulfills his role in God's plan with complete trust and faith.

John

In John's Gospel, Jesus's death is his moment of victory. He reigns from the cross. Jesus is in total control. He lays down his own life, and then he picks it up again (John 10:18). His death is a sacrifice he makes willingly.

In John's Gospel—and only in this one Gospel—Jesus dies as the Passover, or Paschal, lambs are being slain. Jesus becomes the Paschal Lamb, "the lamb of God who takes away the sin of the world" (John 1:29). Not just any lamb could be a Paschal Lamb. It had to be perfect, without any blemish. Only such a lamb was acceptable to God as a substitute for human life. Christians believe that Jesus, too, was perfect, in the sense that he was without sin.

JESUS'S RESURRECTION

On the Sunday after his death, Jesus's followers discovered his tomb empty. After he made appearances before some of them, they became convinced that he had risen from the dead. The resurrection renewed the disciples' faith in Jesus as the Messiah. It also gave them great joy and strengthened them.

Jesus was not, of course, the only example of someone rising from the dead. Word had spread that Jesus had raised several people from the dead, including his friend Lazarus. Many centuries earlier, the prophet Elijah had brought a widow's son back from death. Resurrection was not an unusual idea in Jesus's day, either. True, the Sadducees rejected the notion, but the Pharisees and many other Jews firmly believed in the resurrection of the dead. The only real surprise was that Jesus rose alone. Most people had been expecting a general resurrection of all the dead to mark the end of the age.

It is hard to assess the immediate impact of Jesus's resurrection on the disciples. The Gospels imply that Jesus used his post-resurrection appearances to continue instructing his followers. The Apostles did not gain the courage to teach and preach from the resurrection alone, however; they only begin to do those things after their personal baptism in the Holy Spirit at Pentecost.

Minimally, the resurrection must have assured the disciples that Jesus was not an imposter. God did not raise up false prophets or evildoers. God had set his seal of approval upon Jesus. God had also offered a stern rebuke to those who had accused Jesus of blasphemy and claimed that he deserved to die. According to God, Jesus had deserved to live.

3

Scriptures

And the book of the prophet Isaiah was handed
to Him. And he opened the book, and found
the place where it was written: "The Spirit of
the Lord is Upon Me, Because He has anointed
Me to preach the gospel to the poor...." And he closed
the book, and gave it back to the attendant, and sat
down, and the eyes of all in the synagogue were fixed
upon Him. And he began to say to them, "Today
this Scripture has been fulfilled in your hearing."

—Luke 4:17–21

THE HEBREW BIBLE (OLD TESTAMENT)

The Bible of the earliest Christians was the Hebrew Bible. (The Hebrew Bible is the set of writings that Jews call "the Bible" and Christians call "the Old Testament.") When the writers of the New Testament refer to the Scriptures, they almost always mean the Hebrew Bible.

In 2 Timothy 3:16, the Scriptures are described as inspired by God and useful for instruction. Why would the author of 2 Timothy make a point of this?

Around the year A.D. 150, a crisis developed in the Christian movement. Marcion, a Christian leader who taught in the city of Rome, concluded that the Hebrew Scriptures were incompatible with a belief in Jesus. He chose to discard them entirely. The writer of 2 Timothy may have been addressing (and arguing against) an earlier version of this attitude.

The Christian Church rejected Marcion's position, and included all thirty-nine books of the Jewish Bible in the Christian Bible. Christians, however, interpret these books in a different manner from Jews.

From earliest times, Christian preaching included the claim that the Hebrew Scriptures pointed to the coming of Jesus (see, e.g., Peter's Pentecost speech in Acts 2, and the beginning of the Gospel of Matthew, where five Hebrew Bible verses are applied to Jesus: 1:23, 2:6, 2:15, 2:18, and 2:23). This made it necessary to read the Scriptures in a nonliteral sense, for no section of the Hebrew Bible speaks about Jesus directly. This was not unusual; everyone used nonliteral interpretations at that time. The difference was that Jews saw the words of Scripture as being fulfilled in the lives of the Jewish people, while Christians believed that the Scriptures were fulfilled in Jesus. For example, to Jewish interpreters, the suffering servant song in Isaiah 53 referred to the suffering of the Jewish people in general. Likewise, the story of Abraham's near-sacrifice of his son Isaac (Genesis 22) foretold the slaughter of Abraham's children and the near-extinction of the nation in times of catastrophe (e.g., the fall of the northern kingdom of Israel to the Assyrians in 721 B.C., the Babylonian conquest of Judah in the early sixth century B.C., the reign of Seleucid ruler Antiochus IV Epiphanes in the second century B.C., and the destruction of Jerusalem by the Romans in A.D. 70). Christians, on the other hand, saw Jesus as the suffering servant, and they believed that Abraham's sacrifice prefigured God's sacrifice of his own son, Jesus.

THE LETTERS OF PAUL

Paul was an outsider who became the most successful preacher of the Jesus movement. He never knew Jesus during Jesus's lifetime, though he claimed to have seen him after the resurrection. Before he became part of the Jesus movement, Paul had hunted down and killed the followers of Jesus.

Paul was a realist. He knew that the Jesus movement could stir up messianic expectations, leading to political rebellion. He also knew that any insurgent activity would bring swift and brutal retaliation from Rome. Paul was not wrong. Zealot activity around the year A.D. 70 led to a massacre in Jerusalem and the destruction of the Temple. In 135, the Bar Kochba revolt resulted in many Jews being killed and the rest being forced to leave Jerusalem.

Paul was also a zealous Jew. In his mind, the Jesus movement was not true Judaism. Paul was a Pharisee. The Law was, in his eyes, the heart of Judaism. Although it was the Romans who crucified Jesus, it was Jews who had handed him over to them, so he must have been guilty under the Law. That said, he could not have been God's Messiah. Case closed. All things considered, Paul must have felt fully justified in attempting to destroy the Jesus movement.

All of Paul's death-dealing clarity regarding right and wrong, true and false, crumbled when he encountered the risen Jesus. "For the letter kills, but the Spirit gives life," Paul would later write (2 Corinthians 3:6), reflecting, perhaps, upon his own earlier zeal for the Law and how it had led him to oppose the followers of Jesus.

Paul's encounter with the risen Jesus utterly transformed his life. He became a leader in the Jesus movement, claiming the outreach to the Gentiles as his special mission. He founded Christian communities in many cities in Greece and Asia Minor. After Paul left a community, he would keep in touch with it by means of letters. Many of the letters of Paul found in the New Testament are of this nature.

Paul's letters usually address specific concerns within particular communities. Nonetheless, it is obvious that certain themes recur in his letters, and are central to his thought. The process by which we can discern the outlines of Paul's thinking is somewhat akin to the process by which we distill the philosophy of a politician from the many speeches he has given on different occasions.

Paul's transformation included a radical change in his thinking. He came to believe that people were not so much in need of someone to enforce the Law as they were in need of someone to free them from the bondage of sin. If the Law were enforced, people would die, for sin is deserving of death. What people needed was not for God to be a lawgiver, judge, and executioner, but for God to be a savior. Paul believed that, in Jesus, God was acting to save sinners. God did not wish to condemn and destroy his creation, but to give it a second birth. Paul called the regeneration of humanity in Jesus "the second Adam," and he called the renewal of the world "the new creation."

To die with Christ, Paul said, was to die to sin (Romans 6:2–3). To rise with Christ was to become a member of his body, to serve Christ rather than sin with the members of one's own body. Just as the wife and husband did not own their own bodies, but belonged to each other (1 Corinthians 7:4), so it was between the Christian and Christ. Christ surrendered his body for the sake of those who believed in him (Ephesians 5:25). Likewise, believers themselves died and surrendered their bodies to Christ so that Christ might live in them (1 Corinthians 6:15). It was a relationship so intimate that only the conjugal metaphor seemed appropriate for it (Ephesians 5:31–32).

Everyone who accepted this type of relationship with Jesus became part of the body of Christ, another name for the

Church. Each congregation was to be a community bound together in love, in which people served one another with the gifts individually given to them by the Holy Spirit.

Paul's letters always contain a section on ethics, but his system of ethics is not based on the Law. Those who are led by the Holy Spirit do not need to be concerned about the demands of the Law (Galatians 5:18), for the whole Law is summed up in the command to "love your neighbor as yourself" (Galatians 5:14). Those led by the Holy Spirit will manifest the fruits of the Spirit (love, joy, kindness, and self-control, among others); against such there is no law (Galatians 5:22–23).

THE GOSPELS

The New Testament contains four Gospels: Matthew, Mark, Luke, and John. Each of them tells the story of Jesus's life, death, and resurrection. Though they have many elements in common, they are not the same. Each Gospel begins and ends in its own way, and each offers a unique selection and arrangement of stories about Jesus.

The stories themselves had been treasured and passed on orally for a generation or more before becoming incorporated into one or more of the Gospels. Each of the four Gospels paints a unique portrait of Jesus by weaving together different parts of the oral tradition.

Although they are usually referred to as "the Gospel of Mark" or "Luke's Gospel," the Gospels are actually anonymous writings. The names were added by the early Church. No one knows for sure who wrote the Gospels. Most scholars believe each was the product of an entire community of believers, not just an individual author. That said, I will still use the convenient shorthand way of referring to them.

The Gospel of Mark

The first verse of the Gospel of Mark announces that it will be telling "the good news of Jesus Christ, the Son of God." The Greek word for "good news" used here, *euangellion*, actually means "a good announcement" or "a happy proclamation." It was used when news of victory was brought back from the battlefield. It seems to be an appropriate word to use, since Jesus was victorious over Satan, as evidenced by the large number of exorcisms in this Gospel. When Jesus's jealous rivals charge that he can cast out demons only because he is in league with Satan, the chief demon (Mark 3:22), Jesus responds with a parable about a strong man and a thief who wants to rob him. Even if the strong man were your friend, would he stand idly by if you

WHERE DID THE NEW TESTAMENT COME FROM?

The New Testament is the second part of the Christian Bible. It is the most important part of the Bible for Christians.

The New Testament began its process of formation as soon as people began to pass on stories about what they had seen Jesus do or heard him say. This occurred even during his lifetime. The process of passing on a person's words and deeds by word of mouth is called "oral history." The New Testament began as oral history.

Most of the twenty-seven books of the New Testament appeared in written form sometime in the second half of the first century, between A.D. 50 and 100. Paul's letters were the first to appear, and 2 Peter and Revelation were among the last.

The process of canonization (deciding which Christian writings would be included in the New Testament and which would not) was mostly completed by the end of the fourth century, although Revelation was not accepted in the East until as late as the tenth or eleventh century.

The original language of the Jewish Scriptures (the first part of the Christian Bible) was Hebrew, and that of the New Testament was Greek. St. Jerome (c. 347–420) translated the entire Christian Bible into Latin around 400. Some people think that this was to keep it out of the hands of the ordinary people, but actually, Latin was the common language at the time, and that was the reason for Jerome's translation. Few ordinary people read the Bible because first, they could not afford to purchase one, and second, they could not read.

The Bible was first translated into English in the fourteenth century by John Wycliffe. The King James Version appeared in 1611. Most modern English Bibles use the King James Version as one of their sources.

started stealing his possessions? The answer, of course, is no. You must first tie up the strong man, says Jesus, and then you can rob his house (3:27). The fact that Jesus is able to free people from the power of the demons proves that he has already tied up Satan. That is why this Gospel is a victory announcement of good news.

In the first section of the Gospel (through 8:21), it appears that nothing can stop Jesus. The crowds are amazed at the authority of his teaching (1:22, 27). Jesus heals so many people that he can no longer enter a town without being mobbed (1:45). Even his disciples are awestruck when he stills a storm at sea. They exclaim, "What manner of man is this, that even the wind and the sea obey him?" (4:41). The crowds are "astounded beyond measure." "He has done all things well," they say, "even enabling the deaf to hear and the mute to speak" (7:37). However, something even more incredible is about to happen.

In the central section of Mark's Gospel (8:22–10:52), Jesus announces his approaching suffering and death three times. This man who seems to be a paragon of power is about to undergo pain, humiliation, and death. In an amazing show of blindness and deafness, Jesus's disciples not only fail to hear what he is telling them, but squabble over which of them will be greatest in the Kingdom of God (10:35–37). They are not ready to acknowledge the sacrifice that Jesus is about to make, let alone willing to follow him.

Because they were not ready to hear and to follow, Jesus's disciples all abandoned him when he was arrested and executed. Only the women who used to follow him and provide for him were present at his crucifixion, and even they stood at a distance (15:40–41). These same women discovered the empty tomb on the following Sunday morning, and fled in fear. The Gospel of Mark ends at this point, with all of Jesus's followers hiding and silenced.

Recall the first verse of Mark's Gospel: This was supposed to be good news. Is it? It didn't end the way people wanted it to, with Jesus on a throne and those who had followed him proven right in their faith. On the other hand, if you believe the claim of the

Gospel that salvation is present despite the blindness, obstinacy, hard-heartedness, and fear that surrounds it, then it *is* good news!

The Gospel of Matthew

Matthew's Gospel contains much of the material found in Mark, and also some additional information. The largest block of new material is the Sermon on the Mount. The theme of the Sermon on the Mount is greater righteousness. This part of Matthew's Gospel challenges followers of Jesus to follow a way of perfection that exceeds the demands of the Law.

Scholars believe that the Gospel of Matthew was written to oppose another group of Jews, a coalition of Pharisees who had the same basic goal in mind. Neither Matthew nor this group of Pharisees was content to do the minimum—that is, just to carry out the letter of the Law. Both believed that the fulfillment of the Law was nothing less than a life lived entirely in obedience to the will of God. They differed only in the method by which they thought human beings could be led to live such a life.

The Pharisees believed that God had provided the answer to the quest for holiness in Mosaic Law. As custodians of the Oral Law, which sought the correct application of Mosaic Law in every generation, they worked diligently and prayerfully to stitch together a way of life that Jews might wear as a garment no matter where they lived. This task was especially important after the Temple was destroyed in A.D. 70, for the Temple had been the place where God's holiness dwelt, and where human beings could draw close to it.

The author or authors who wrote the Gospel of Matthew also believed that the destruction of the Temple marked an important new era in Jewish history, one in which human beings would have to seek the holiness of God in a new way. They believed that God had provided that new way in Jesus. They believed that Jesus, and Jesus alone, was the fulfillment of the Law, because only Jesus had lived a life of total obedience to the will of God. Matthew's Gospel portrays Jesus as the supremely obedient one.

Matthew's Gospel also depicts the life of Jesus as the culmination of Jewish history. In the Gospel, Jesus retraces the footsteps of ancient Israel: He is called out of Egypt (2:15), he is a survivor of a massacre (2:16, 20), he is tempted by Satan in the wilderness (4:1), and he is obedient to the prophets of God (3:13). In addition, he is the fulfillment of the Scriptures (see, e.g., 1:23, 2:5–6, 2:17–18, 2:23, 4:12–16). Only Matthew provides so many Scripture passages that Jesus is said to have fulfilled.

The reader of Matthew's Gospel is led to see Jesus (and his followers) as the true Israel, as the culmination of Jewish history and Mosaic Law. The implied contrast is with another group of Jews that also claimed to be the true continuation of ancient Israel and the custodian of Mosaic Law.

The Gospel of Luke

Luke's Gospel focuses on Jerusalem. It begins with the prophet Zechariah in the Jerusalem Temple. It is the only Gospel to place Jesus in the Temple both for his presentation as an infant (Luke 2:22), and at age twelve when he was found visiting with its teachers (2:46). Approximately ten chapters out of twenty-four (9:51–19:28) are devoted to Jesus's journey to Jerusalem. In the remainder of the Gospel, Jesus teaches in Jerusalem (often specifically inside the Temple), is arrested and crucified there, is buried there, and rises from the dead there. Luke's Gospel begs the question: Did Jesus really spend such a great percentage of his life in Jerusalem? Probably not, because all the other Gospels center his ministry in Galilee, with only rare journeys to Jerusalem.

Luke is not interested in the precise chronology of Jesus's life, however, but in the purpose for which he lived. When Jesus sets his face toward Jerusalem (9:51), he is accepting his fate. Jesus, whose compassion for sinners was well known, would himself be treated as a sinner. Luke writes his Gospel to show that this end was not an unforeseen tragedy, but the whole reason for Jesus's life. It was part of God's plan. To read

Luke's Gospel is to follow Jesus as he heads toward Jerusalem, and to learn from him how to love God and to love one's neighbor as oneself. This is to be "on the way," one of Luke's favorite metaphors (13:22, 14:25, 17:22) for following Jesus. As disciples travel with Jesus along the way, they grow in understanding.

In Luke's writings (Luke also wrote the Acts of the Apostles), the Apostles are the link between Jesus and the Church. They are the "eyewitnesses" (Luke 1:2) on whom Luke relies for his account. Hence, Judas Iscariot, who betrays Jesus and then commits suicide, must be replaced by someone who was with Jesus from his baptism by John the Baptist to his ascension into heaven (Acts 1:22). Luke also includes women among the eyewitnesses. Indeed, it is from the story of Martha and Mary (Luke 10:38–42) that we learn that watching and listening to Jesus is the one thing necessary. Such watching and listening enable one to be a witness to Jesus, another important concern for Luke.

Luke shows Jesus praying more often than any of the other Gospel writers. Luke also mentions the power of the Holy Spirit far more than does any of the other evangelists. This is true both in Luke's Gospel (see, e.g., 1:35, 4:1) and in Acts, which, in addition to numerous references to people being "filled with the Holy Spirit" (e.g., Stephen in Acts 7:55), includes the famous account of the Holy Spirit descending upon some of Jesus's closest associates at Pentecost (Acts 2).

Luke's Gospel emphasizes Jesus's compassion. All of society's marginalized—women, the diseased, Samaritans, Gentiles, sinners—beseech Jesus at every turn for help. Some of their problems are physical, some social, and some psychological. No matter what the nature of the complaint, Jesus can and does try to heal it. Three of the parables found only in Luke— the good Samaritan (10:29–37), the prodigal son (15:11–32), and the rich man and Lazarus (16:19–31)—drive home the importance of compassion for the injured, for sinners, and for the poor.

The Gospel of John

John structured his Gospel around a paradigm of descent and ascent. In the first half of the Gospel, Jesus descends from the Father into this world, where he performs miracles and teaches. In the second half, beginning with chapter 13, Jesus reascends to the Father. He instructs his disciples in private, suffers and dies, and appears to his followers after his resurrection.

Everything in the Gospel points toward understanding that Jesus is the word of God, which is sent forth from God and does not return empty. It accomplishes that for which it was sent (Isaiah 55:11). Through his word, God reaches down into the world to redeem it.

Everything Jesus does and says reveals his true nature and glory. Yet people do not recognize who Jesus is because they are from "the below" while he is from "the above" (John 8:23). Jesus has come from the Father, and does the works of the Father. Yet, despite the testimony of his words and works, the leaders of the people do not know where he is from (9:29).

In the first half of the Gospel, Jesus changes water into wine (2:1–11), heals those who are paralyzed (5:2–9) and blind (9), multiplies loaves of bread and fishes (6), offers streams of living water from his heart (7:37–38), identifies himself as the good shepherd who lays down his life for his sheep (10:11), and raises Lazarus from the dead (11). Each of these episodes is a sign of things to come in the last half of the Gospel. Through his death and resurrection, the wine and rejoicing of the Kingdom of God will be released. The spiritually paralyzed will be empowered, and the spiritually blind will see. Jesus's body will be sacrificed as food for the world. His side will be pierced, and from it will flow living water. He lays down his life, and takes it up again. In the Gospel of John, there is less tension between Jesus's miracles and his death than there is in Mark, because the miracles prefigure his death.

Jesus's crucifixion is, ironically, his exultation. It appears to be the moment at which the Jesus movement fails, but it is actually the moment at which Jesus, having accomplished the purpose for which he was sent, ascends to God the Father.

OTHER NEW TESTAMENT WRITINGS

The Gospels and the Letters of Paul are the two largest blocks of material in the New Testament. The New Testament also contains a history of the early Church (Acts of the Apostles), the Letter of James, the Letter of Jude, two letters of Peter, three letters of John, and a symbolic, visionary book known as Revelation. The interpretation of Revelation is hotly debated, with some claiming that it refers entirely to events in the first century A.D., others insisting that it contains a prophetic account of the end of the world, and a third group saying it provides a description of the situation of the Church in all times and places.

4

Worldview

*. . . He said to them, "Thus it is written,
that the Christ should suffer and rise
again from the dead the third day;
and that repentance for forgiveness of sins should
be proclaimed in His name to all the nations,
beginning from Jerusalem."*

—Luke 24:46–47

THE STRUGGLE TO DEFINE JESUS

When a religion is born, it dislodges the accepted worldview of the day and age and generates its own, new worldview. Every religion is born of a revelation or an insight that creates its own context, because it would make no sense in the original context. All new religions generate their own language because they need to speak about something that cannot be spoken about using the verbal coinage previously at their disposal.

For Christianity, that which could not be understood within the old context was Jesus. Jesus broke all the molds, including the religious molds, of his time. This required his followers to create a new worldview, cultural context, and language. This new worldview is what we now call Christianity. The Christian Bible was at first the product of this newly emerging worldview, and later, the authoritative source of it.

In this chapter, we will consider the main outlines of the Christian worldview. I will focus on those aspects of the worldview that are unique to Christianity. Therefore, although the ideas of creation and the Last Judgment are very important to Christians, I will not highlight them here, since the Christian idea of creation does not differ substantially from that of Jews and Muslims. Likewise, Jews, Christians, and Muslims all believe that there will be a judgment at the end of the world, although in this concept there is at least one important difference. Jews, Muslims, and some Christians believe that this judgment will involve weighing a person's good and bad deeds. Other Christians, however, believe that people will be judged on the basis of their beliefs, not their deeds. These Christians say that only those who believe in Jesus will enter heaven.

"WHO DO YOU SAY THAT I AM?" (MARK 8:29)

After Jesus taught the crowds and performed many miracles, he queried his closest companions to see what they understood from his words and deeds. "Who do you say that I am?" he asked. Peter, the burly, spontaneous spokesperson for the group, responded with the greatest designation of honor that a first-century Jew could bestow upon a human being: "You are the Messiah!"

While there was a great deal of disagreement among first-century Jews as to the exact job description of the Messiah, everyone agreed that the Messiah would be someone appointed by God to make right everything that was wrong with the world. In the eyes of those who believed in him, Jesus certainly fit that description. Therefore, in a sense, Peter's answer was right. However, as the ensuing conversations recorded in Mark's Gospel make clear, Peter did not have a very solid grasp on who Jesus was. Neither did any of the other disciples. That is because Jesus broke the mold. In the long run, Christians decided that Jesus was the Messiah, but he was also much more. Ultimately, Christians decided that Jesus was both God and human. This did not happen without a struggle, because Jews do not accept the idea of a god-man, and the first Christians were originally pious Jews.

The Gentiles, who became believers in large numbers beginning around A.D. 50, *did* have a concept of a god-man. Actually, they had two sources for this concept. One derived from Greek mythology, which said that a god-man would be a person born of the union of a human being and a deity. This concept did not fit what Christians wanted to say about Jesus for a few reasons: First, the Gentiles had many gods, but Christians were committed to the concept of one God. Second, mythological god-men were born by means of a sexual union between a human woman and a god, but Christians did not believe Jesus was conceived in that way. Third, a god-man was considered *less* than god, because his human heritage "diluted" his divine nature. He was only half god. This is not what Christians wanted to say abut Jesus.

The second Gentile source for the concept of a god-man was the deification of the emperor. The Romans bestowed upon several of their emperors the honor and titles that were normally reserved for the gods. However, Jesus, unlike the emperors, sat upon no worldly throne, and received humiliation rather than honors.

The ultimate reason why none of the Gentile concepts seemed appropriate for Jesus was that the Gentile concept of God was in no way as exalted as the Jewish concept of God, and Christians wanted to retain the Jewish notion.

There was *no* concept that expressed what Christians wanted to say about Jesus. They had to invent it.

Christians decided that Jesus was both the one God of the Jews *and* a real human being. Trying to explain how that could be took about four centuries of work, culminating in the Council of Chalcedon in A.D. 451. Even then, it was impossible to explain completely how someone could be at the same time both the infinite, eternal God, and a finite human being who is born and dies.

The first written expression of the coexistence of divine and human in Jesus is in the opening chapter of the Gospel of John. There, John speaks of God's word becoming flesh.

DEFINING THE UNITY OF GOD AND HUMAN IN JESUS

Therefore, following the holy Fathers, we all with one accord teach men to acknowledge one and the same Son, our Lord Jesus Christ, at once complete in Godhead and complete in manhood, truly God and truly man, . . . of one substance (*homoousios*) with the Father as regards his Godhead, and at the same time of one substance (*homoousios*) with us as regards his manhood; like us in all respects, apart from sin; as regards his Godhead, begotten of the Father before the ages, but yet as regards his manhood begotten, for us men and for our salvation, of Mary the Virgin, the God-bearer (*Theotokos*); one and the same Christ, Son, Lord, Only-begotten, recognized in two natures, without confusion, without change, without division, without separation; the distinction of natures being in no way annulled by the union, but rather the characteristics of each nature being preserved and coming together to form one person and subsistence (*hypostasis*), not as parted or separated into two persons, but one and the same Son and Only-begotten God the Word, Lord Jesus Christ. . . .

Source: From the Definition of Chalcedon (451)

God's word is coeternal with God, and it is God's presence in the world. The Christian Church assigns both of these attributes to Jesus. John says that God's word became flesh in Jesus. Later Christians would say, "God became man in Jesus." This Christian belief is called the *Incarnation,* a term that means "becoming flesh." The Christians' belief that they had seen God in Jesus led not to a new God, but to a new understanding of the traditional God of the Jews.

THE TRINITY

When Christians began to say that Jesus was God, they did *not* mean that God had vacated heaven. Jesus himself, after all, prayed, "Our Father who art in heaven . . ." Presumably, he would not have done so if God was no longer in heaven, but only in Jesus's own person on Earth.

Christians believe that Jesus left Earth when he ascended into heaven. However, they also believe that the Holy Spirit was given to them by Jesus, and will remain with them through the ages. But if both the Father and Jesus are in heaven, how can God also be present on Earth?

As they reflected on questions like these, Christians began to speak about "God the Father," "God the Son," and "God the Holy Spirit." Initially, these may have been no more than ways to talk about their various experiences of God. First, they recognized God as transcendent, as someone who, although not a part of the world, was the source of everything that makes up the world. This is "God the Father."

Second, they knew God through what was begotten by him, or born of him. Birth is an amazing thing—one person suddenly becomes two. Christians believe that God begot Jesus through all eternity, not only at a particular moment in time. They also believe that Jesus, unlike other children, never set himself against

And the Word became flesh and pitched a tent in our midst . . .
—John 1:14

his father's will. What God willed, Jesus willed, too. Such a child, although a separate person from his parent, is nonetheless the perfect image of the parent. One can see the parent in the child. Christians called this view of God in Jesus "God the Son."

Finally, Christians experienced God dwelling within themselves. It was God who empowered them, enlightened them, and set them free. Christians called this power of God rising up within them "God the Holy Spirit," and they believed that the Holy Spirit was a gift given to them because of what Jesus had accomplished on Earth.

Eventually, Christians would define "God the Father," "God the Son," and "God the Holy Spirit" as three separate persons within the one and only God. So, when Jesus prayed, he was not addressing an empty heaven, but God the Father. And even though God the Father and God the Son might reside in heaven, God the Holy Spirit can nonetheless remain with Jesus's followers on Earth throughout the ages.

SIN

Every religion believes that life is not what it could or should be. Every religion believes that there is something wrong with the world, something that can be made right. Religions do not simply report on what is. They are transformative—that is, they try to change things.

The Christian word for what is wrong with the world is *sin.* Christians believe that the world should be in accordance with God's will. God's will is holy, and all that conforms with it is holy as well.

The opposite of holiness is sin. The Bible says that God wants people to be holy, as he is holy (Leviticus 19:2). Christians do not believe that we are born holy, however. We are born innocent but not holy. Innocence is a lack of acquaintance with sin. It is inexperience with sin. Innocence is a beautiful thing, but it is not the same thing as holiness. Both holiness and innocence imply a lack of wrongdoing. However, a holy will is one that actively opposes sin, not one that is blissfully ignorant of sin's existence.

The Christian doctrine of original sin says that all people are born in sin. This does not mean that sin is part of our nature, because our nature is inherently good and holy. Like everything else in the world, human beings are created by God, and Genesis 1 states that God pronounced all that he had created good.

Nonetheless, experience shows that sin is somehow inbred in us. We do not simply sin because we freely choose to do so. The Christian idea of sin is not limited to willful maliciousness. We sin despite our best efforts. This is the Christian way of stating the dilemma of the world. We do not live as God intends us to live, nor can we on the basis of our own efforts. In and of ourselves, we do not have the capacity to live holy lives. We are geared toward sin, not toward sanctity. The classic statement of this dilemma is found in Paul's Letter to the Romans (7:14–25).

Sin is the Christian word for all that is wrong with the world. It refers to far more than personal wrongdoing. Every kind of suffering, and every other evil in the world, is connected to sin. Suffering is not necessarily the result of personal sin. The first Christians certainly knew of Job, the righteous sufferer of the Bible. They also knew of the "suffering servant" of God in Isaiah (52:13–53:12), who personally bore the sins of others. However, even though those who suffer are not necessarily guilty of sin, Christians still believe that suffering is always the result of sin. In the Christian worldview, suffering is not an accident. Sometimes it is a punishment for personal wrongdoing, but not always. Often it occurs because God has laid on the sufferer the sins of others (Isaiah 53:4, 6, 10–12).

> I am of the flesh, sold into slavery under sin. I do not understand my own actions. For I do not do what I want, but I do the very thing I hate. . . . But in fact it is no longer I that do it, but sin that dwells within me. For I know that nothing good dwells within me, that is, in my flesh. I can will what is right, but I cannot do it. For I do not do the good I want, but the evil I do not want is what I do. Now if I do what I do not want, it is no longer I that do it, but sin that dwells within me.
>
> **—Romans 7:14–20**

To say that we are born in sin is not only to say that something is wrong within individuals, but also that something is wrong in the world all around us. There is no apparent justice. The wicked may prosper, and the innocent may be put to death. There is suffering that results from economic dislocation, a social order that privileges some at the expense of others, or perhaps from a lack of education or opportunity. This suffering is often said to be the result of "corporate sin" (meaning the sin of a whole group of people, rather than individual sin) or "social sin" (meaning sin that arises from the workings of society rather than from the intentions of individuals).

Conservative Christians often emphasize personal sin, and liberal Christians often emphasize corporate or social sin. Both ideas of sin, however, are part of the Christian worldview.

REDEMPTION

Christianity offers what initially appears to be an unduly dramatic answer to the problem of sin: the sacrificial death of the son of God. One might think that the answer to the problem of sin should be no more complicated than issuing a prophetic call to repentance; those who chose to heed such a call would turn away from sin and beg for God's forgiveness. One would think that God, being compassionate and merciful, would readily grant forgiveness.

Actually, this *is* the way sin is handled on a day-to-day basis in the lives of most Christians. However, sin may only be handled this way on the assumption that the covenant between God and humanity is intact. One cannot go to someone and ask for forgiveness if one no longer has a viable relationship with him or her.

Consider, for example, a child who disobeys its parents. As long as the child is a part of the household and family, the child need simply ask for forgiveness for its wrongdoing and promise not to continue on its wayward path, and all is resolved. The strained relationship between child and parents is healed.

In a more radical situation, however, these steps may not suffice. Imagine that the child leaves home and, being without any source of income, hires on to work as a prostitute or drug dealer. Or, suppose that the child, without its parents' protection, is captured and sold into slavery. (This was once a common practice, and it still happens today in some parts of the world.) In either case, although the child may feel sorry, it cannot ask for forgiveness because it is separated from its household and family. Nor can the parents simply go find their child and take it home, for someone else now holds the legal right to the child's labor. The child is "estranged" from its parents—the family ties have been broken. Authority over the child now belongs to a criminal or a slave dealer. Though the child has slipped the bonds of his parents' authority, he or she has no freedom. The child's deeds and decisions are not his or her own.

Christians believe that something similar happened between God and humanity. God made several covenants with humanity. He had made a special covenant with Abraham and his descendants, and more general covenants with Noah and Adam that applied to all people. Christians believe that all of those covenants were broken. By the time Jesus was born, humanity was estranged from God. Not only the covenant with Adam, but even the covenant with Abraham, had been broken. After claiming that the Gentiles refused to honor the God they knew through creation (Romans 1:20–21), and that the Jews had failed to obey the law God had given them (2:17–24), Paul concluded that "all, both Jews and Greeks, are under the power of sin" (3:9).

In this dire situation, can sinners simply turn to God and ask for forgiveness? They cannot, because the covenantal relationships that provided for forgiveness of sins do not exist anymore. By their own choice, human beings are no longer under the authority of God. They are estranged from God; they have moved out of God's household. They no longer enjoy the possibilities open to those who belong to God's family and have a close relationship with God.

In developing this picture of the dire circumstances of humanity, Christians were drawing on biblical passages that portrayed God as Israel's husband, and Israel as God's unfaithful wife. After graphically detailing the long history of Israel's unfaithfulness, which led to the broken covenant (Ezekiel 16:59), Ezekiel speaks of a new, everlasting covenant that will come with God's forgiveness (16:60, 62–63). Christians believe that Jesus brought that new covenant. Jesus overcame humanity's estrangement from God and allowed God to forgive the sins of Jews and Gentiles alike.

In order for human beings to be forgiven and brought back into God's household, they needed to be "redeemed." To *redeem* means "to buy back" or "pay off someone's debt." Human beings were (metaphorically) sold into prostitution, bondage, and slavery. Someone else had legal rights over them. So God needed to redeem them—that is, God needed to buy them back or pay off their debt. Christians believe that Jesus paid the price of humanity's redemption by giving up his life for theirs.

Just as God offered the earlier covenants out of love, to espouse human beings to himself, so Jesus, having purchased humanity as a result of his love for people, becomes the bridegroom. All those who enter into the marriage covenant with him are his bride. Therefore, Christians speak of the Church as "the bride of Christ." Being married to Jesus makes one a child of God, because Jesus is God's son. Christians see themselves as God's "children-in-law." Because Jesus paid the price for their lives—purchased them and married them—they are brought back into God's family. We have a new life; we are a new creation. Their old lives, mired in sin, are no more. This is what Christians sing about when they go to church on Sunday morning. This is why they praise Jesus.

5

Visiting Christian Churches

We, therefore, following the royal pathway and the divinely inspired authority of our Holy Fathers and the traditions of the Catholic Church (for, as we all know, the Holy Spirit indwells her), define with all certitude and accuracy that just as the figure of the precious and life-giving Cross, so also the venerable and holy images, as well in painting and mosaic as of other fit materials, should be set forth in the holy churches of God....

—Decree of the Second Council of Nicea, 787

C hristian communities have traditionally gathered for worship on Sunday morning. Whereas Jews celebrate the Sabbath from Friday evening to Saturday evening, Christians celebrate it on Sunday, the day of the week on which Jesus is believed to have risen from the dead. Seventh-day Adventists are an exception to this rule. They believe that Jesus did nothing to warrant changing God's original command regarding celebrating the Sabbath on the seventh day of the week, so they celebrate the Sabbath on Saturday. It should also be noted that many Christian churches have recently begun to offer services on Saturday or Sunday evening, or even on another day of the week, either to accommodate people's busy schedules or to offer additional opportunities for worship. Catholic churches offer Mass every day.

Christian worship varies greatly in style. Certain elements, however, are usually present: prayer, music and song, readings from the Bible, a sermon, and the Lord's Supper or Holy Communion. A priest or a minister presides over the gathering, and the members of the congregation stand or sit facing the presider. Church furnishings typically include pews (benches with backs) or other seating for the congregation, an area for the choir and musicians, a lectern for Bible reading and preaching, and a table or altar for communion.

The architecture of a Christian church building varies with location, climate, and denomination. Some church buildings are built in a grand, ornate style. Congregations that build such churches want to glorify God by lavishing attention on God's home. They sacrifice the money required to build a grand structure to show that God is the center of their community.

Other churches are purposefully simple in design and furnishings, avoiding what their communities consider empty pomp and display. Christians who build simple churches are demonstrating their desire to keep the focus on God and the hearts of people, rather than on material things.

Churches usually have a cross conspicuously displayed somewhere. Traditionally, the cross was perched on top of a high tower known as a "steeple." Contemporary church buildings may have a cross painted on an exterior wall or set up as a piece of sculpture on their grounds. In the past, churches themselves were usually designed in the shape of a cross. Today, the cross is a culturally accepted symbol of Christianity. In the Roman Empire, however, Christian use of the cross was a counter-cultural act. The Romans used the cross as an instrument of torture and humiliation for criminals. To glory in the cross, as Paul did (see Galatians 6:14), would be to revere an executed criminal, and to risk the wrath of the empire for questioning its system of justice.

Orthodox and Catholic church buildings are often named after saints. This is less common among Protestant Christians, although some denominations (such as Lutherans and Anglicans) do name their churches after saints.

We turn now to an examination of some of Christianity's many styles of worship. Worship is the highlight of the week for a Christian of any persuasion, so it is not surprising that we will discover here great beauty, enthusiasm, reverence, intellectual rigor, and spiritual depth, though not necessarily all in the same church.

ORTHODOX WORSHIP

The independent national Churches of Orthodoxy derive much of their unity from a unique form of worship that they hold in common. It is called the Divine Liturgy. A "liturgy" is a set form of prayer. It is not spontaneous. In liturgical worship, most prayers, responses, and actions are the same from Sunday to Sunday.

Orthodox worshipers are not bored by the repetition. Rather, they say it is essential to the purpose of the Divine Liturgy. Just as a gymnast may perform a particular skill a thousand times before perfecting it, or a pianist play a song countless times before it becomes effortless, so it is with prayer. Words will only sink deep into our hearts and transform our consciousness through constant repetition. If a person likes a song, it is no chore to repeat it over and over. It is a delight. Finally, the song becomes so much a part of the singer that it bubbles up and can help sustain the person in times of trouble. This is what the Divine Liturgy is designed to do. It is intended to become so much a part of the believer that he or she will live it from day to day, and be shielded by it in times of distress.

The Divine Liturgy is a *ritual*—a set of words and actions that are believed to be divinely ordained and established. From this perspective, it is not up to human beings to decide how they will worship. God provides the form of worship, and human beings are expected simply to follow it.

Orthodox theology emphasizes the holy mystery of God. God cannot be seen with the senses or known by the minds of human beings. Orthodox worship focuses on that holy mystery, offering a form through which mystery can be adored.

Although words from the Bible and concepts from theology are evident in the liturgy, neither is offered for intellectual stimulation. Almost all of the words used in the liturgy are chanted or sung, which, the Orthodox believe, drives them into the soul rather than into the mind alone. Even the sermon was sung at one time, though that is not usually the case any longer.

The altar area is shielded from view by an iconostasis, a screen decorated with icons. Orthodox Christians consider these special devotional paintings windows through which the sacred becomes visible. They are closely connected to the mystery of the Incarnation that rendered the invisible God visible. Thus, Orthodox Christians reason, a refusal to venerate an icon is, in effect, a denial of the Incarnation.

Orthodox Christians do not worship icons, they venerate them (show great honor to them). Icons are carried in procession. People bow in front of them, kiss them, and place lighted candles before them. The Seventh Ecumenical Council (A.D. 787) described the veneration of icons as a form of love and worship that is due to God who became flesh.

The Divine Liturgy in the Orthodox Church is close to three hours in length. It can be subdivided into three main parts. In the first, the communion elements are prepared. This section of the service recalls Jesus's birth, or God's Incarnation. The second part includes readings from the Bible, prayers, the sermon, and the Great Procession. In the Great Procession, the communion elements are brought out, symbolizing Jesus's coming forth to teach and to heal. The third part is the communion service itself during which the priest consecrates the elements, then places the bread into the chalice of wine. This portion of the service symbolizes Christ's sacrifice for the salvation of the world. Orthodox Christians believe that the bread and wine actually become the body and blood of Christ.

Traditional Orthodox worship does not include musical instruments. Singing is usually unaccompanied chant. Instrumental and choral music is avoided out of a fear that it may become a "performance," enticing worshipers to focus on human talents rather than on God.

As mentioned above, the Divine Liturgy is a ritual. Rituals involve actions as well as words. Among the actions performed by Orthodox Christians during the Divine Liturgy are walking in procession, making the sign of the cross, and carrying in the book for the readings and the bread and wine for communion. The Orthodox say that mouth and mind are only a part of prayer; complete prayer must also include bodily actions.

Orthodoxy maintains the ritual dimension of its worship as a way of emphasizing its belief that it is embodied existence that will be transfigured in the resurrection. To strip worship of its ritual dimension would reduce it, believers say, to mere words or inward feelings. Despite their love for the Bible, Orthodox worshipers would feel that something important was missing in a service that emphasized the sermon.

Early in the liturgy, the deacon says to the priest, "It is time for the Lord to act." The stress in an Orthodox service is not on hearing the word of God, but on what God *does*. The word of God became flesh, died, and rose again so that human beings might be transfigured and become like God. The effective operation of Christ in the sacraments, the effectiveness of grace in changing us—this is the emphasis of Orthodox spirituality. It is action-oriented, not word-oriented. The action of the Holy Spirit in the Divine Liturgy changes the bread and wine into the body and blood of Christ. The operation of the Holy Spirit in our lives renews in us the image of God. The action of the Holy Spirit in the cosmos renews all of creation.

CATHOLIC WORSHIP
Much of what has been said about Orthodox worship applies to Catholic worship as well. Catholic worship is liturgical; like Orthodox worship, it follows an established pattern of words and deeds. It is a ritual that includes sacred actions.

Most of the differences between Orthodox and Catholic worship are minor. Catholic churches do not have icons, but they often contain paintings, sculpture, and designs on stained glass windows. Gregorian chant was used in Catholic churches until recently, but Catholic music also allows choral singing and instruments.

Catholic spirituality is sacramental. A sacrament is a sign of the sacred. It is, on the one hand, an ordinary object or action, but, on the other hand, it is the locus for the meeting and commingling of divine and material realities. Like the icon, it is an expression of Christian belief in the Incarnation. Just as the sacred word of God in the Bible is the vehicle by which God's will is carried out, so in a sacrament the material reality and human actions are the vehicles through which God's grace transforms those who receive it in faith. Augustine (354–430), one of Chistianity's most influential theologians, even referred to a sacrament as "a visible word," implying that it, too, was a communication from God.

Catholics are less suspicious of human nature and human action than many types of Protestants are. This is a result of their sacramental worldview. As Catholics see it, the divine infusion into the material and human world does not obliterate the physical reality that contains it, but renders it holy, just as God's word became flesh not to destroy human nature but to make it holy.

The Eucharist (literally, "thanksgiving") is a ritual action that recalls both the Last Supper and Jesus's death on the cross. At the heart of the ritual is the consecration of the bread and wine. The bread and wine are changed into the body and blood of Christ as the priest pronounces sacred words and performs sacred actions. Jesus, present on the altar, offers himself to God the Father as an unbloody sacrifice that is nevertheless the same sacrifice as the one offered two thousand years ago on Mount Calvary (the place outside Jerusalem where Jesus was crucified). To understand how this can be, we need to know that ritual places the participant in the sacred realm, an eternal realm where time as we know it does not exist. (This is as true of Jewish ritual, or Native American rituals, or any other religious ritual, as it is of Christian ritual.) In a ritual, past, present, and future exist simultaneously. Catholics believe that this is what happens during the sacrifice of the Mass. The believer is truly present at Calvary as Jesus offers himself in sacrifice (past), is part of the present worshiping community, and is also given a foretaste of heaven, where he or she will one day sit at a table with Jesus and all of the saints (future). Taking communion is a preview of the heavenly banquet.

The Catholic Mass has two main parts: the Liturgy of the Word and the Liturgy of the Eucharist. The first focuses on the reading and explanation of the Scriptures, the second on Jesus's loving sacrifice and his giving of himself as spiritual nourishment. The reading of the Scriptures and the sermon are kept separate—that is, the presider does not interject his own comments into the passages from the Bible. Ideally, the reading takes place in the style known as *lectio divina* ("divine reading"), a prayerful style of reading developed in the monasteries. In lectio divina, the Scriptures are read slowly and reflectively, with pauses, giving the listener time to sense God's presence and take in his words. Not only the bread and the wine, but the Scriptures, too, are spiritual food. The sermon, which follows the readings, applies the lessons found in the Scripture readings to the contemporary lives of the congregation.

The culmination of the Mass is not found in words, however, no matter how prayerful the reading or inspired the sermon. Like the Orthodox Liturgy, the Catholic Mass focuses on the *action* of Christ, on what Christ *did* for humanity. The greatest lesson of all is learned from the sacrificial death of Christ, not from the readings or the sermon. The greatest love of all time is the love of Christ. According to the Gospels, when Jesus walked on Earth, no one wanted to follow him to Calvary. In the Mass, however, Catholic Christians do precisely that—they stand witness to Jesus's act of self-sacrifice. It is only because of his sacrifice that they are able to receive his body and blood during the part of the Mass known as "communion." Catholic Christians believe that since God was pleased to show his love for the world in this way, they should be present there. That is why most Catholic churches offer Mass not just on Sundays, but daily.

PROTESTANT WORSHIP

The sense that the church building is the house of God, the spot where heaven and Earth meet and where God's throne may be approached by mere mortals, is less pronounced among Protestant Christians than it is among Roman Catholic and Orthodox Christians. Protestants tend to view the church as the gathered fellowship of believers. It is the meeting of people to hear the word of God preached, and to support each other in their Christian way of life. Consequently, in the eyes of Protestants, "the church" is not primarily a building, but a gathering of believers.

Protestant worship emphasizes the importance of the sermon, which is generally the focal point of the service. The sermon will explain one or more passages from the Bible. Protestants disagree, however, on the best way to interpret the Bible. A minister may make use of an interpretive framework based in Lutheran or Calvinist theology. Alternatively, he or she might describe the historical or social background of the text(s) in an effort to aid the congregation's understanding. Other ministers pride themselves on preaching from "the Bible alone." Those who take the latter course believe that theological, historical, and social concerns may distort the meaning of the text. They, in turn, have been criticized for a lack of attention to context. Preachers who use academic frameworks believe that academic training is the only safeguard against importing one's own ideas or cultural assumptions into the text.

Unlike Orthodox and Catholic churches, Protestant churches are not united in a single institution or under a single human head. Consequently, Protestant Christianity is more diverse. This is reflected in worship styles. Here we are able to mention only a few of the distinctive elements of different kinds of Protestant worship.

A BAPTIST SERVICE

Baptist worship is less standardized than that of many other denominations, because Baptist churches do not have to answer to a bishop or a governing body beyond the local level. Rather than attempt to generalize about Baptist worship, I will describe a Baptist service that I observed.

I visited a church named Bethel Baptist, located in a Midwestern city with a population of around 18,500. Bethel Baptist has a semicircular arrangement of pews. Its decorations are simple but contemporary in style. Most of the decorations are artistic renditions of verses from the Bible. The central area, where the musicians perform and the minister preaches, reminded me of a stage. Suspended from the ceiling on either side of this central area are two billboard-size screens. There is no altar.

The worship service began with music. The singing was spirited and enthusiastic; the words were projected on the large screens. There were drums, a keyboard, and a guitar. The music was Jesus-centered, emphasizing that Jesus is our connection to God, that he alone shows us what God is like, and that it is he who enables us to stand in God's presence. Sometimes the music had an emotional tinge; the refrain of one song proclaimed, "no one can touch my heart like you do."

The creed was sung, not spoken. This Baptist congregation belted out a creed in echo style (the congregation repeating a phrase after the musicians), with instrumental accompaniment, lots of rhythm and

In marked contrast to Orthodox or Catholic worship, a Baptist service is neither a liturgy nor a ritual. There are no established patterns of worship that are held to be sacred. This means that Baptists are able to adopt modern technology and contemporary musical styles with an ease unimaginable in a liturgical church.

Not all Protestants are nonliturgical. Martin Luther retained many elements of Catholic worship. Today, Lutheran churches have an altar, candles, vestments, and other elements that many other Protestants have discarded. Like Catholics, they refer to their service as "the Eucharist" or even "the Mass." The order of the prayers is very similar to that in the Catholic Mass. The two

beat, and some handclapping. It is easy to see why this style of worship would be popular with young people, but the older adults seemed to be enjoying it, too.

I arrived on the day when the pastor was beginning a new series of messages based on the Sermon on the Mount (Matthew 5–7). Pastor Dennis Erickson spoke about our spiritual poverty (or the lack thereof)—that is, the lack of our willingness to mourn over our own sins, as David did in Psalm 51. Erickson questioned whether evangelical Christians (and it was clear that he included his congregation among them), in their passion to clearly proclaim Christ's triumph, had not made light of the reality of sin in their lives.

Pastor Erickson knows the Bible well, and he preached it with an eye toward guiding contemporary evangelical culture by it. This Baptist pastor attended a seminary, and appeared both well-educated and well-read. (Baptist pastors are not required to attend seminary, but a local church may stipulate that it will not call a minister unless he has a seminary education.)

Bethel Baptist called Erickson to its pulpit twenty-seven years ago, and has trusted his leadership ever since. I was curious about what Baptists would look for in a pastor, so I asked members of the congregation what they most appreciated about Pastor Erickson. They mentioned two things above all else: (1) he does not confuse the Bible with his own opinions, and (2) he is morally above reproach.

main subdivisions of the service are "The Liturgy of the Word of God" and "The Eucharistic Meal" (recall that the two main subdivisions of the Catholic Mass are "The Liturgy of the Word" and "The Liturgy of the Eucharist"). Lutherans are known for their contributions to church music. Prolific classical composer J. S. Bach, for example, was Lutheran. Lutherans supported the use of the organ in church when others thought it was too closely associated with secular music. Martin Luther himself was a notable hymn writer. He is probably best known for his "A Mighty Fortress Is Our God." In contrast with many other Protestant churches, where the pulpit vastly overshadows the communion table, Lutheran worship gives nearly equal attention to the proclamation of the word and the sacrament of communion.

Anglicans worship with a service that may be called either Holy Eucharist or the Mass. Like the Lutheran Eucharist, it is very similar to the Catholic Mass. Anglicans have seven sacraments, and, like Catholics, they believe that the sacraments operate as "visible signs and effectual means" of God's grace at work in people.

Fundamentalist and Pentecostal services, on the other hand, are nonliturgical and nonsacramental. It is difficult to generalize, since many of these are independent churches, but the services I observed contained two main parts: worship in song and the sermon.

Traditional Quaker worship is different from all the types of worship discussed so far. There is no presider, and no program to follow. Instead, participants sit in quiet prayer or meditation, speaking when they feel moved by the Holy Spirit to do so.

Jehovah's Witnesses meet in Kingdom Halls (not churches). There, they spend most of their time in Bible study and discussion.

Mormon temples are the site of unique rituals, which are closed to non-Mormons. Members of the Church of Jesus Christ of Latter-day Saints (the official name of the Mormon religion) do not go to temple on a regular basis, however.

Temple services are reserved for special occasions. On Sunday mornings, Mormons worship in local churches or chapels, and their services there are very similar to Protestant services. They sing hymns, pray, listen to a sermon, and share concerns and testimony. Mormons also have a weekly sacrament meeting where communion is served, using bread and water rather than wine (Mormons do not drink alcohol).

6

Growing up Christian

And they were bringing children to Him so that He might touch them; and the disciples rebuked them. But when Jesus saw this, He was indignant and said to them, "Permit the children to come to Me; do not hinder them; for the kingdom of God belongs to such as these."

—Mark 10:13–14

BAPTISM

Christians officially enter the Church by being baptized. In baptism, water is used as an outward sign of cleansing from sin and the person's new life in Christ. How the water is applied varies. Some Christians sprinkle the person being baptized. Others pour water over the head. Baptists require a full immersion in a tank, stream, or lake. In popular parlance, Christians may "sprinkle, pour, or dunk."

With only a few exceptions, Christians are baptized "in the name of the Father and of the Son and of the Holy Spirit" (Matthew 28:19). One of the exceptions is the rapidly growing United Pentecostal Church, which baptizes members in the name of Jesus only. Most Pentecostal churches, including the very large Assemblies of God Church (with 32 million members worldwide), baptize in the name of the Father, Son, and Holy Spirit. The United Pentecostal Church International has approximately 2.6 million members worldwide.

At what age a person should be baptized is a controversial issue among Christians. Orthodox, Catholic, and many Protestant Christians baptize babies. All Christians also baptize adults, but some Christian churches do not baptize infants. Baptists, Mennonites, Hutterites, and Mormons do not baptize anyone until the person is old enough to understand the faith and make his or her own personal commitment to it.

The most common argument against infant baptism is that the New Testament mentions only adults being baptized, never infants. It is true that the New Testament only gives the *names* of adults who were baptized, but it would have been rather unusual to give the names of children for any reason in that era. The New Testament mentions the baptism of an entire family several times (e.g., 1 Corinthians 1:16, Acts 10:2, 48). No indication is given of the ages of the children in these families. Consequently, we do not know whether any infants were among the first generation of baptized Christians.

Baptism is an important event in any Christian's life. It is the means by which one officially joins the Church.

LEARNING TO PRAY

Most Christians memorize the Lord's Prayer, and many memorize the Apostles' Creed. Beyond that, Christians have few formal prayers in common. Families often pray with their children at mealtimes and at bedtime. Some families use memorized prayers at these times, while others pray in an extemporaneous manner.

Pentecostals may pray in tongues, or utter prophecies. Though they may be psychlogically prepared for this by seeing other people do it, they do not learn how to pray in this style through study or practice. Pentecostals minimize human direction so as to leave the channels open for the Holy Spirit to move freely.

The Orthodox Liturgy and the Catholic Mass, on the other hand, are long, memorized, corporate prayers. These are not individual prayers, but the prayer of the Church as a whole. Their very form is believed to be not only ancient and hallowed by age, but also sacred and hallowed by God, and therefore invariant.

Orthodox and Catholic Christians also say individual prayers. A young person once explained to me that her religion was different from her friend's (Catholic) religion because she believed that she could pray directly to God. When I explained to her that Catholics usually prayed directly to God as well, and that the priest was

THE LORD'S PRAYER

Our Father in heaven,
hallowed be your name.
Your kingdom come.
Your will be done,
on earth as it is in heaven.
Give us this day our daily bread,
And forgive us our debts,
as we also have forgiven our debtors.
And do not bring us to the test
but save us from evil.

—Matthew 6:9–13

necessary only for the saying of the Mass and for the confession of sins, she was genuinely surprised.

Catholics pray the rosary, a circlet of sixty beads (including the crucifix). On each of these beads a prayer is recited: the Apostles' Creed once, the Lord's Prayer six times, the Hail Mary fifty-three times, and the Doxology (a prayer of praise to God) six times. At the beginning of each "decade" (a cluster of ten Hail Marys), an event from the Gospel is recalled and meditated upon.

While it is not exactly a form of prayer, Protestants often gain spiritual nourishment from private readings of the Bible. Protestants were the first to translate the Bible into modern European languages, and to place the Bible in the hands of the ordinary believer.

SACRAMENTAL MILESTONES

Among Catholics and Orthodox Christians, the reception of the sacraments is an important event. In Orthodox churches, infants receive the sacraments of baptism, chrismation (anointing with

THE APOSTLES' CREED

I believe in God, the Father almighty, creator of heaven and earth.
I believe in Jesus Christ, his only Son, our Lord.
He was conceived by the power of the Holy Spirit and born of the Virgin Mary.
He suffered under Pontius Pilate, was crucified, died, and was buried.
He descended to the dead.
On the third day he rose again.
He ascended into heaven, and is seated at the right hand of the Father.
He will come again to judge the living and the dead.
I believe in the Holy Spirit,
the holy catholic Church,
the communion of saints,
the forgiveness of sins,
the resurrection of the body,
and life everlasting.

oil), and communion. Young people make their first confession when they are old enough to understand the concept of sin and its reality in their lives. Among Catholics, the first taking of communion and the sacrament of confirmation are postponed until after a child's first confession.

Penance

The sacrament of penance or reconciliation is often called "going to confession." Preparation for one's first confession involves learning to recognize one's own sins, and allowing oneself to feel sorrow for them. God's grace is believed to be present in the sacrament, offering the help that is needed for improvement.

The person receiving the sacrament confesses his or her sins to a priest, who is sworn to secrecy. A priest is strictly forbidden to repeat anything he hears in confession. The person receiving the sacrament will be asked to express sorrow for the sins confessed by saying a prayer. The priest will then pronounce the words of absolution, which assure the person of God's forgiveness of his or her sins. Finally, the priest will assign some prayers to be said, or perhaps assign another way to make amends to God and the persons harmed by the wrongdoing that was confessed.

In the Gospel of John (20:23), Jesus gives his disciples the power to forgive or refuse to forgive sins. The Catholic and Orthodox churches believe that Jesus intended this power to be passed on to the spiritual descendants of the disciples through all ages.

Communion

Catholic and Orthodox Christians believe that Jesus is truly present in the sacrament of communion. In a mysterious way, the person privileged to receive communion shares in the body and blood, the very life, of Christ. His or her body becomes like a temple or a tabernacle, a place where God dwells on Earth.

In Catholic worship, people go to the front of the church to receive a wafer of unleavened bread and a sip of wine. In Orthodox churches, adults receive communion in much the same way.

Recall that the Orthodox, unlike Catholics, allow infants to take communion. The priest places a spoon containing a small bit of wafer soaked in wine in their mouths.

Catholic girls very often wear a special white dress for their first communion, and boys usually wear a suit. In Catholic churches, the first reception of communion takes place when a child is around seven or eight years old. Catholic families will often celebrate a child's first Holy Communion with religious gifts and a meal.

Chrismation or Confirmation

Orthodox children are anointed as infants. This sacrament is called chrismation. The similar Catholic sacrament of anointing is called confirmation. The age at which a Catholic is confirmed varies, but it usually occurs sometime during the middle school or high school years. In this sacrament, a person makes a mature decision to accept the faith and the teachings of the Church, and receives the gifts of the Holy Spirit. The gifts of the Holy Spirit (wisdom, understanding, counsel, fortitude, knowledge, piety, and fear of the Lord) provide what one needs in order to carry on the work of Christ. This sacrament also bestows the strength necessary to be a faithful witness to Christ.

The sacrament is usually administered by a bishop. The bishop will question the people who wish to be confirmed, testing their knowledge of their faith. Since young people typically spend a year or two in preparation for this sacrament, they are generally well equipped for this test. The bishop will then lay his hands on their heads, anoint them with blessed oil, and strike each person on the cheek (to remind them that Christians must be ready to suffer for their faith).

MILESTONES IN NONSACRAMENTAL CHURCHES

Even churches that do not consider confirmation a sacrament may nonetheless see it as a milestone in a person's life. Many Protestant churches baptize infants, and most of those that do offer a ceremony of adult confirmation of one's faith for young people who are ready to make that affirmation. There is no set age for this ceremony, but the average age is probably around twelve or thirteen. There will usually be a year or more of instruction in the faith preceding confirmation.

Something similar might be said of the first participation in the Lord's Supper (Holy Communion). Even where it is not a sacrament, it is an important event, and may be marked by a luncheon in honor of the young person who has attained that stage of maturity.

Some Protestants view their progress through the various levels of Sunday school or Bible camp as important milestones. One young Presbyterian whom I interviewed remembered that all third-grade Sunday school students received a Bible as a gift from the church.

In those churches that emphasize a conversion or "born again" experience, having that experience is certainly an important moment in a young person's life. Many people think of being born again as a dramatic experience. It can be, but it doesn't have to be. Ruth[9], who is a Baptist, a mother, and a youth leader, explained it this way: "People need to realize that they need Christ. People are sinners, and God cannot accept sin into heaven. Jesus paid the price for our sin. This is the Gospel message. When you accept the truth of it, and invite Christ into your heart, and make him Lord of your life, you are born again."[10]

On the other hand, a member of the Reformed Church in America told me, "I was raised as a child of the covenant, meaning that I was baptized as an infant and it was assumed that God loves me, chose me, and has wonderful plans for me. I can honestly say that I have never had a conscious time in my life when I did not know God, perhaps in an analogous way that I do not remember recognizing that my mother is my mother—it always seemed to be so."[11]

FAMILY

The types of experiences that young Christians have obviously depend to a great extent on the type of family in which they grow up. Those who are active Christians as adults often give much of the credit to their families. Tamera Schreuer, wife of a Reformed Church pastor, said she remembered that her parents "integrated their faith into our daily lives. They did this through daily Bible readings and devotions, talk, but mostly, I think, what impacted me was their actions.

"My parents practiced hospitality and service out of a deep love and care for others that was an extension of the love God has for us," Tamera explained.

> My dad was always helping to fix things at the Church or school, or at a needy person's home. My mom always had cookies available for anyone who stopped by, for anyone who needed a caring ear, or to take to someone who was needy. We took in foster children and loved them to pieces during their brief or long stay as part of our family. My parents were not known as the most educated or highest ranked, but I rate their hearts as the biggest in how they cared. To this day they dedicate their retirement years to go on weeks and months of volunteer service with the Red Cross, Wycliffe Bible translators, or CRWRC (a disaster relief agency).

Tamera then related how she could see this Christian lifestyle continuing from one generation to the next. After seminary, she and her husband "boldly raised our children while doing inner city ministry work in the New York City metropolitan area. Our children know what it means to bring the love of God to others and receive God's blessings from others, even from those who on the outside look very needy." [12]

Rachel, a college student, grew up in another kind of Christian home. Her mother is Presbyterian and her father is Catholic. Both her mother and her father decided that their own church was important enough to them to stay with it, even though that meant attending different churches. Rachel and her brother went to the Presbyterian church with their mother. On Christmas and Easter, however, the entire family worshiped together. Rachel remembers that, on one such occasion, someone said to her, "I didn't know you had a dad." At first, she felt confused, then hurt, by the remark. Eventually, she realized that the speaker simply hadn't realized that there was more than one kind of Christian family. Her parents had made an uncommon choice, but Rachel believes it was a good one. As she reflected on her experiences growing up in her Christian home, she concluded that they had made her "more open-minded." She feels fortunate to have learned that two people don't have to agree on everything, even in the very important realm of religion, in order to bless each other with the love of God and be blessed in return.[13]

Of the many people I talked to about growing up Christian, no doubt the one who had faced the most challenging experiences was Sharon, a Lakota Indian. Sharon's family had been Catholic for many generations. She attended an integrated Catholic grade school for eight years. In that school, Indian children were discriminated against by students and by teachers because they were poor and came from a Native American background. They were made to feel like second-class citizens.

Sharon attended a Catholic boarding school for Native Americans during her high school years. Her parents could not afford to send her to the Catholic school in the city where they lived. They did, however, manage to find the money to send her to a very fine boarding school run by the Benedictines (a Catholic religious order).

Sharon recalled that she and her classmates attended Mass every morning and benediction every night. She felt that she received a very good education there. There were good meals, and her relationships with her classmates were happy ones. "There was some discipline," she said, "but not overly so." The only discrimination she noticed took place between students. Although Sharon is not a full-blooded Indian, she did notice that full-bloods were often picked on.

The real problems involving her Christian beliefs arose when Sharon was living on the reservation. In the last quarter to half century, there has been a strong resurgence of interest in Native American religions. Sharon participated in sweats and other native religious rituals. She came away from those experiences believing in the strong power of the ceremonies. There is no doubt in her mind that native religion works. "You went in with a problem and came out with an answer," she said. "The medicine men have real contact with their spirit helpers, and they can truly heal all kinds of things."

Still, even though she has experienced their power, Sharon has decided to remove herself from all native religious ceremonies. The Pentecostal church that she currently attends believes such practices are evil.

The encounter between Christianity and native religions on the reservations has resulted in a situation that Sharon describes as "confusing." She identifies strongly with being Lakota and recognizes the centrality of the traditional ceremonies to Lakota identity. At the same time, she wants to grow in her Christian faith, and she respects its exclusive claims. At least for the time being, she has decided to put aside the Lakota ceremonies and pursue her relationship with the Christian God.[14]

EDUCATION

Sharon's story brings us to the important topic of education. Christian education runs the gamut from Sunday school and catechism classes to denominationally supported private schools and homeschooling. We will examine each of these aspects of Christian education.

Sunday School

Generations of Protestant Christians can remember going to Sunday school.[15] Few, however, know the history of this institution.

In the British Isles, in the first half of the eighteenth century, a number of Puritan, evangelical, and Quaker congregations taught Bible reading and basic skills on Sundays. This development was an outgrowth of the Reformation emphasis on direct access to the Bible for all people. Such direct access required, obviously, the ability to read. But many people, especially the poor, were illiterate. So Christians began to teach people to read. Adults as well as young people attended these classes.

History has credited Englishman Robert Raikes (1735–1811) with the founding of the Sunday school movement. Raikes was the editor and proprietor of the *Gloucester Journal*. One day, he and the Reverend Thomas Stock, a Quaker, were watching some children play in the street. Both the children and their parents worked long hours every day in a nearby pin factory. There was no time for school, and there were no compulsory education laws. The children, who had little guidance from parents or teachers, were swearing as they played. The pastor and the editor agreed that a special school might be a good way to provide "proper direction and guidance" for children like these, children whose parents were among what today would be called "the working poor." Because the classes met on Sunday (the one day of the week when the children were not working), they came to be called "Sunday schools." Robert Raikes established a school for the children of chimney sweeps in 1780. This was the first official Sunday school.

Raikes used his position at the *Gloucester Journal* to advertise the Sunday school classes, sending the movement off to a rapid start. Soon cities were reporting attendance in the thousands for these classes. In 1785, the nondenominational Sunday School Society was established to coordinate and develop the schools. England's first Sunday schools attempted to improve the lives of the poor by teaching them reading and writing, telling Bible stories, and seeing that they received baths and decent clothing.

The English Sunday school movement spread to the United

PASTOR RECALLS CHILDHOOD SUNDAY SCHOOL

In looking back on my spiritual formation, I recognize the importance of the weekly experience of Sunday school. Sunday school classes featured lessons in Bible knowledge and interpretation plus large group activities of spirited singing, recognition of birthdays and, once in a while, special speakers such as a missionary from Africa.

—Reverend Edward Schreur,
Pastor of Faith Reformed Church

States. In 1790, Benjamin Rush established the first Sunday school in Philadelphia. Rush was a Universalist (someone who believes that all people are saved). He was also a signer of the Declaration of Independence, and he founded Dickinson College, a nationally known and highly selective liberal arts college located in Carlisle, Pennsylvania.

The first meetings of Rush's Sunday school were attended by William White, an Episcopalian bishop who had served as chaplain of the Continental Congress during the American Revolution, and Matthew Carey, a Roman Catholic and publisher. Rush, White,

HANNAH MORE'S SUNDAY SCHOOL

Famed philanthropist Hannah More (1745–1833) was part of the Clapham Sect, a group of wealthy evangelicals who sought to rekindle fervor in the Church of England. They were opposed to slavery and committed to missionary work. In 1789, Hannah and her sister Martha More opened their first Sunday school in Cheddar. More than a dozen additional Sunday schools would be established by the two sisters over the following decade.

Hannah More is famous for her contributions to Sunday school pedagogy. The Mores strove to incorporate entertainment and variety into their classes. Lessons were carefully designed to suit the level of the students. Hannah believed that singing could increase energy and attention span. As an evangelical, she believed that children are not innocent, but rather have "a corrupt nature and evil dispositions." However, she also thought that children responded much better to kindness than to terror. In many ways, Hannah More was very progressive for her day.

On the other hand, the schools founded by the More sisters did not teach reading and writing to the working classes. Hannah would not allow it. Like many people of her time, she believed that if the poor learned to read and write, they might become disobedient to their masters or engage in sedition against the government.

Hannah used the Bible to support the traditional social order, in which everyone knew his or her place and did not resent it. The poor were expected to be submissive. Hannah wrote extensively; one of her literary goals was to open people's eyes to the foolishness of notions such as liberty and equality.

and Carey founded what were known as First-Day Schools and the First-Day Society. In 1824, the First-Day Society became the American Sunday School Union. Although African Americans founded their own Sunday schools, it is worth noting that some of the first Sunday schools in the United States were open to all children, regardless of race.

Richard Allen was a pioneer of African-American Christianity in the United States. He founded the African Methodist Episcopal Church. In 1796, the trustees of this church, "having a great desire to give our children and brethren instruction in reading the Scriptures,"[16] passed a resolution authorizing a first day school to be held in their meeting house. Some scholars believe this was the first African-American Sunday school, but others give the honor of founding the first one to Katie Ferguson, a poor African woman who is said to have established the first Sunday school in New York City in 1793, reportedly with no knowledge of the work of Raikes or other Sunday school organizers.

By 1851, three-quarters of all working-class children were attending Sunday schools. The degree of influence of Sunday schools on the great reform movements of the nineteenth century (including abolition, temperance, and women's rights) can only be estimated, but it was undoubtedly substantial.

Catholic Schools

The Roman Catholic Church operates the most extensive Christian school system in both the United States and the world. The Lutheran Church–Missouri Synod operates the second largest Christian school system in the United States. Many other denominations also have private Christian schools. Although the number of Catholic schools has declined over the past thirty-five years, the Catholic school system has served as the prototype for Christian schools.

The U.S. Catholic School System

In the United States, the National Catholic Educational Association (NCEA) operates some eight thousand Catholic schools. Of this number, 6,785 are elementary schools and 1,215 are secondary schools. The NCEA is the largest private professional education organization in the world.

In 2003, approximately 2.5 million students, or 5 percent of the total school age population in the United States, were enrolled in Catholic schools. Slightly more than half of these students (51.6 percent) live in the Mideast and Great Lakes regions. However, the Southeast and Western regions have been experiencing enrollment increases, while the Mideast and Great Lakes regions have had slight enrollment declines over the past ten years.

Minority students account for slightly more than a quarter of the enrollment in Catholic schools. Non-Catholic students represent 13.4 percent of the total enrollment. Non-Catholics may attend a Catholic school because their families are appreciative of the discipline afforded by these schools, or they may be attracted by the strong academic performance of Catholic school students. On standardized national tests, private school students generally outperform public school students, and Catholic school students have consistently outperformed even other private school students. The low pupil/teacher ratio (16:1) is also attractive to many.

Catholic schools attain their impressive test results at a lower per pupil cost than that of public schools ($5,571 per student at the secondary level and $3,505 for an elementary school student, as compared to an average cost of $7,284 for a public school student), although approximately two-thirds of those expenses are paid by the parents of the student, while public education is paid for by tax money. Consequently, even though Catholic school tuition is a financial burden for the families who enroll their children there, Catholic schools save the nation almost $18.6 billion a year.

The Catholic school system attempts to include children who come from poor families. Some 45.2 percent of Catholic schools are located in urban and inner-city areas, despite population decreases and the financial challenges involved in maintaining those schools.

These glowing statistics would not be possible without the dedication of the teachers (who often accept lower salaries than their public school counterparts) and the monetary support of the nation's Catholics.

History of Catholic Schools in England

Christian schools predated the first public schools. In Europe, during the Middle Ages, education was entirely under the control of the Church. In 1410, a judgment rendered by the Lord Chief Justice of England asserted that education was the Church's business; it did not come under the jurisdiction of common law. The justification for this decision was that the education of children was a spiritual matter.[17]

The Reformation brought educational upheaval in its wake. Nations continued, for the most part, to assign educational responsibilities to the church, but now there was more than one church. One or another denomination was the established church, and the other churches were considered "nonconformist" or "dissenting." Dissenting churches often objected to having their youth educated in a system designed by the established church. This is not surprising. After all, they were "dissenting" because they disagreed with the established church.

In England, the established church was the Anglican Church. All schools were placed under Anglican control, and the right to teach was restricted to Anglicans in good standing. Catholics were among the dissenting Christians in sixteenth-century England. They were forbidden to attend Catholic schools. Anti-Catholic legislation passed in 1581 made it high treason to reconcile with the Catholic faith. Schoolteachers who were absent from the (Anglican) parish church on Sundays or holy days were subject to a year in prison.

In the seventeenth century, the rift between England's established church and its dissenting churches widened. This was the century in which the Puritans, another group of English dissenters, gained control of the government and then, upon losing it, fled in large numbers to America.

By the eighteenth century, the Industrial Revolution was transforming English life dramatically. Cities were filled with growing numbers of poor and illiterate factory workers. This was also the age of the French and American revolutions, and large numbers of people were fearful that England's poor might stage their own political upheaval. Consequently, when Catholics and others began to establish "charity schools" to provide education for the urban poor, they faced resistance from those who thought that education should be restricted to the politically stable upper classes.

Charity school organizers persisted despite opposition. By 1803, there were ten such schools. French Catholic clergy, fleeing the atheistic French Revolution, helped to staff them.

It was not until 1829 that English Catholics were emancipated. In 1850, the Catholic hierarchy was restored. Catholic elementary schools were legal by 1870, but conditions were appalling. They served mainly the poor. Teachers faced poor attendance and low salaries. Because of inadequate pay, teachers lived in the very worst areas, right alongside the poor people they served. There was a high mortality rate among male Catholic teachers. Approximately fourteen out of every hundred men who were teachers died at a relatively young age, usually from consumption (tuberculosis).

It was only by virtue of their willingness to make great sacrifices that the Catholic working class in England increased the number of its schools from 350 in 1870 to 1,066 in 1902. Catholic parents believed that the Board schools (the equivalent

FAMOUS ECONOMIC PHILOSOPHER OPPOSES SCHOOLS FOR THE POOR

Charity-Schools, and everything else that promotes idleness and keeps the poor from working, are more accessory to the growth of villainy than the want of reading and writing, or even the grossest of ignorance or stupidity.

—Economic philosopher Bernard Mandeville, 1723

of U.S. public schools) housed a latent, if not overt, anti-Catholic atmosphere.

In 1902, England established a dual system, supporting both Board schools and Dissenting schools. This system endured, although it came under frequent attack because of the administrative inconvenience of maintaining two different school systems. It would seem that the Catholic school system has succeeded in England, despite the initially strong opposition to Catholics in that country after the Reformation.

Homeschooling

Homeschooling has become increasingly popular over the last several decades. The 1999 report of the National Center for Educational Statistics (NCES) indicated that 850,000 students, or approximately 1.7 percent of the total school age population in the United States, is homeschooled. In that same year, *Education Week*, a publication covering K–12 issues, reported that at least one million students were being homeschooled. Some estimates claim that the number is actually closer to 1.23 million students, which would mean that 2.5 percent of the total U.S. school age population is being homeschooled.

Homeschooling is legal in all fifty states. In 1996, the U.S. Congress decided that parents do not need to have a teaching certificate in order to homeschool their children.

Homeschooled students generally score exceptionally high on standardized achievement tests, on a par with students in private schools. It should be noted, however, that only about 20 percent of homeschooled students take those tests.

Despite the name, homeschooling rarely takes place entirely at home. Homeschooled children make use of libraries, museums, certain classes at public or private schools, and correspondence or distance education courses. Homeschooling families may band together to sponsor field trips. Some public schools allow homeschooled students to participate in their extra-curricular activities.

Research on homeschooled children is sparse, but researchers who have studied these children find them to be creative, self-reliant, and focused. They have a more clearly defined sense of who they are and what they want to do than do public school children of a comparable age.

Homeschools are as diverse as families. Some are highly structured, some are unstructured, and others try to find a happy medium. Some use public school textbooks, while others purchase commercial curriculum materials designed for homeschoolers. The creation of instructional materials and self-help books for homeschoolers is a growing industry.

Reasons for homeschooling are also diverse. Some parents feel the public schools are too structured, while others worry about the lack of discipline they see there. Parents may feel that they can provide a more academically rigorous education, or they may wish to individualize their child's education. They may want their child's education to include religious beliefs and values. They may be worried about negative peer pressure. They may feel that education should be a family matter, not a government matter. Homeschooling parents may be members of the countercultural left or of the Christian right, although in recent years the latter has been more common.

I visited with Sue, a mom who homeschools her four children. She was working full-time when her children were young, so she taught them after work. As a beginning homeschooler, she was very structured. She even sent homework along with the babysitter. As she observed the uniqueness of each of her children, however, she began to adapt both the curriculum and the teaching style to each individual child. She finds that her children have needed less structure as they matured. Sue also admits that her own personality factors into the educational equation. She does not enjoy having to adhere closely to a certain process. She prefers to spend most of her time searching for quality educational materials to match each child's needs.

Sue and her husband, Chuck, are conservative Christians who want their children to be aware of Charles Darwin's theory of evolution, but do not want them to base their decisions on it.

They also object to the lack of any mention of God in the public schools. They believe that children need role models and heroes, and are sorry to see that modern history books cannot seem to allow heroes to remain inspiring and untarnished.

When I asked why she did not send her children to a Christian school, Sue replied that, to her, not having other people's values imposed on her children was just as important as the Christian element. "I do not want someone else raising my babies," she told me. Sue and Chuck are part of the back-to-nature movement. Their children were born at home. They milk their own dairy goats and gather eggs from their own chickens. Whenever possible, they avoid the medical establishment and rely on herbs and chiropractic to take care of their physical maladies.

As I listened to Sue explain why she homeschools her children, I discerned four main threads in her reasoning:

- Homeschooling provides an opportunity to deal with the individual learning styles of each child, and to give individual attention to each child.

- We need to teach our children to think, not just teach them to memorize in order to pass a test.

- Our children need to learn about God, and about what it means to put your trust there rather than in science, medicine, or technology.

- Children need heroes and role models. And they need to know that important, successful leaders are not necessarily too proud to kneel and pray.[18]

RELIGIOUS EDUCATION AND RELIGIOUS CONFLICT

The history and contributions of Christian education are impressive. There is a potential negative side, however.

Religious education programs are established with the express purpose of passing on a unique set of understandings, knowledge, and values from one generation to the next. Problems can arise, however, when the desire to maintain uniqueness leads to isolated perspectives.

When religious divisions are never crossed, when neighborhoods and schools are filled with one faith only, interreligious dialogue and understanding are endangered. It is precisely this situation that fosters the continual fighting between Protestants and Catholics in Northern Ireland, and between Israelis and Palestinians in the modern state of Israel. In both of these cases, people have recognized the need for religiously integrated education, and have taken steps to implement it.

This does not mean that religiously segregated education is necessarily bad. It does mean that religious schools need to teach respect and appreciation for the spiritual identity of others, while also forming the religious identity of their own.

7

Christian Cultural Expressions

Let your souls, men, remembering Christ, cry heia!
The Source of Good and Being, the Highest Power,
  Offers the warrior and gives the victor prizes.
Let your souls, men, remembering Christ, cry heia!

—St. Columban, "Boat Song," c. 600

GOD'S GRANDEUR

The world is charged with the grandeur of God.
It will flame out, like shining from shook foil;
It gathers to a greatness, like the ooze of oil
Crushed. Why do men then now not reck his rod?
Generations have trod, have trod, have trod;
And all is seared with trade; Bleared, smeared with toil;
And wears man's smudge and shares man's smell: the soil
Is bare now, nor can foot feel, being shod.
And for all this, nature is never spent;
There lives the dearest freshness deep down things;
And though the last lights off the black West went
Oh, morning, at the brown brink eastward, springs—
Because the Holy Ghost over the bent
World broods with warm breast and with ah! bright wings.

—Gerard Manley Hopkins

Gerard Manley Hopkins was born on July 28, 1844, near London, and died at the age of forty-four in 1889. He was an Anglican Christian who became a Catholic. During his lifetime, he was a moderately successful priest and teacher, and a virtually unknown poet.

"God's Grandeur," his most famous work, begins with an image of God's creative activity, charging the world in the sense both of furnishing it with energy (like charging a battery), and of giving it a command.

The world reflects God's grandeur like shaken foil reflects light: innumerable irregularities reflecting a single source. When shaken awake, they flame forth, fulfilling the purpose for which they were made.

The flame gathers itself into a great fire. Will it cleanse the world in wrath? No! From fire and light playing majestically between heaven and earth, the metaphor descends abruptly to ooze seeping over the ground.

The ooze comes from oil, most likely olive oil, but the word *ooze* evokes the image of a crushed body, oozing blood. Whether oil or blood, how can the crushing be called a gathering to greatness? The full benefit of the olive is available only after it is crushed. Once pressed into oil, it was used by people in biblical times in cooking, lamps, anointing, binding wounds, and perfume. The Christian naturally extends the metaphor to Christ, bruised and crushed to bring forth the blood that provides spiritual food and healing.

Why, asks the poet, do human beings fail to respect God's rod? Is this the rod of punishment? Or is it the "rod out of the stump of Jesse" (Isaiah 11:1)—that is, Christ himself? Either way, the rod is an image of God's rule and authority.

Our attention is next directed away from God's activity and toward the doings of humanity. Generations have trod the earth, destroying the freshness of God's creation, until at last the light of God's grandeur is replaced with the dark smudges and dank smells of human artifice.

The result of all this stomping is bare soil, bereft of its carpet of vegetation. Not surprisingly, we put on our shoes, shielding our feet from the hard ground and sharp rocks exposed by our tromping.

Gone is the joy of the barefoot child, hard at play in God's world. And gone is the sense of standing in the presence of the divine, which requires, of course, unshod feet (Exodus 3:5).

Yet, for all the feet that have trod, the earth continues to put forth its beauty and bounty. For all the evil and pain the human spirit has endured, courageous hearts enshrine faith, hope, and love. Despite the reality of Christ's death, he is alive, and, for all the reality of sin, people, too, are brought from death to life in Christ.

Even though the world has rejected God's law and God's love, God has not abandoned the world. The world remains the nesting-place of God, who, by the power of the Holy Spirit, continues to bring forth a freshly charged creation each morning.

In Hopkins's poem, the world is a canvas covered with the

glory of God, covered with the corruption of sin, covered with the blood of Christ, covered with the new creation. This is the Christian vision, and millions have been stirred by it, though few have voiced it so powerfully.

In this chapter, we will consider the interplay of Christianity and culture. We will look at representative examples of Christian art, architecture, music, and popular culture. Sometimes we will see Christians using art to shape a dominant culture. Other times, as in the case of the African-American spirituals, we will see them challenging the dominant culture even as they build their own alternative form.

EARLY CHRISTIANITY

In the first three centuries of the Christian era, the most impressive religious monuments found in the Roman Empire were temples dedicated to the gods. These structures housed only a statue of the deity; they were not designed to seat a congregation. Sacrifices to the Roman deities were performed on outdoor altars.

Christian houses of worship were usually modest homes adapted to the purpose of housing a congregation by knocking down a wall or two. The second floor of the home would be the site of the communion meal.

In the city of Rome, the most significant Christian monuments of the first centuries A.D. did not aspire even to such modest heights. They were underground networks of burial chambers known as catacombs. Among the remains of their own beloved dead, Christians prayed and worshiped Jesus, the one who had risen from the dead.

There is some evidence that Christians hid in the catacombs during times of persecution: Blocked staircases, secret passages, and concealed entrances and exits have been discovered. After the Edict of Milan (313) ended the persecutions, Christian churches were often built directly above the catacombs.

Although the catacombs were dank and filled with the smell of decomposing corpses, they were not bereft of artistic inspiration.

There was no sculpture, for that would have been too reminiscent of the Roman temples, but there were paintings.

The story of Jonah was a popular theme. Jonah was a prophet who was swallowed by a "whale" (literally a "sea-dragon") that spit him out on shore three days later, safe and unharmed. Christians saw in Jonah a prefiguration of Christ, who rose out of the belly of the earth after three days.

Another favorite theme was the story of Abraham's near-sacrifice of his son Isaac. Christians saw in this story a prefiguration of God's sacrifice of his son, Jesus. The baptism of Christ in the Jordan River was also popular because baptism itself was so important, being the means by which a person was accepted into the Christian faith.

In the very center of the ceiling of the Catacomb of Saints Peter and Marcellinus in Rome is a depiction of Christ as the Good Shepherd. This portrayal of Christ is modeled on pagan predecessors, with one important difference: The pagan shepherd offers his sheep to be sacrificed to the goddess Athena, whereas Christ lays down his own life for his sheep.

In early Christian art, Christ was almost always portrayed as either the Good Shepherd or as a teacher. Jesus was not portrayed as the imperial ruler of heaven and Earth until after Christianity became the official religion of the Roman Empire in the late fourth century.

BYZANTIUM (THE EASTERN ROMAN EMPIRE)

And therefore I have sailed the seas and come
To the holy city of Byzantium
—W. B. Yeats, "Sailing to Byzantium"

In the fifth century A.D., the Roman Empire split into an eastern and a western section. The eastern section was centered at the city of Constantinople (Istanbul, in what is now Turkey), founded by Constantine I in 330. Constantinople was built on the site of the ancient Greek city of Byzantium.

The people who lived there called it "the New Rome" because they believed their civilization was the legitimate successor of the ancient Roman Empire. We now call the entire Eastern Roman Empire "Byzantium." *Byzantine* is the associated adjective; just as anything that pertains to Rome is called "Roman," so anything that has to do with Byzantium is called "Byzantine."

Byzantium was the womb of Orthodox Christianity. It was a theocratic state. Its emperors were believed to be divinely guided. Byzantium was destined to endure as a distinct cultural and political entity for more than a millennium. Western European, Slavic, and Islamic cultures were able to develop their own intellectual flowering only after learning from Byzantine scholars.

The Eastern Roman Empire continued to be ruled by Roman law and political institutions. The elite carried out official communications in Latin, but the populace spoke Greek. In school, students studied the ancient Greek classics in science and medicine, literature and philosophy, and art and rhetoric. Although the Church developed its own literature and philosophy, it looked with favor upon classical learning. Often, only the part of classical Greek learning that was preserved in Byzantine schoolbooks has survived into modern times.

Constantinople benefited from its enviable location at the junction of Europe and Asia. Its merchants grew rich as a result of their control over the trade routes between Europe and the East, and over the sea commerce between the Black and the Mediterranean seas.

Emperor Constantine saw to it that "the New Rome" had a university, two theaters, fifty-two covered walkways, fourteen churches, and fourteen palaces. He imported massive quantities of the best Greco-Roman art from throughout the empire.

Emperor Justinian (483–565), who came to power in the sixth century, ruled most of the lands surrounding the

Mediterranean Sea. He was an ambitious builder. His greatest monument was the majestic domed church of Hagia Sophia (Holy Wisdom), which was constructed in a mere five years (532–537).

Hagia Sophia

> *Above all rises into the immeasurable air the great helmet [of the dome], which, bending over, like the radiant heavens, embraces the church. And at the highest part, at the crown, was depicted the cross, the protector of the city.*[19]
>
> —Paul the Silentiary, "Descriptio S. Sophiae"

Byzantine architects fashioned the largest domes in the ancient world. The most famous example is Hagia Sophia, situated in the city once called Constantinople, but now known as Istanbul, Turkey. As the imperial church, Hagia Sophia was served by 80 priests, 150 deacons, 60 subdeacons, 160 readers, 25 cantors, and 75 doorkeepers.

Hagia Sophia was built in the sixth century, before steel was used in construction. Without steel, heavy roofs had to be supported by massive pillars or walls. The dome of Hagia Sophia was supported by four massive piers, each measuring about 118 square yards at the base. The church itself was 270 feet long and 240 feet wide. The dome, about 110 feet in diameter, soared 200 feet above the floor.

The dome, which represents the vault of heaven, rode on a cushion of light that poured through forty windows in the dome's base. This created the illusion that this massive dome was floating in air. Once admitted through the windows along the base of the dome, the light glanced off mosaics and gold-covered vaulting, played along the jeweled splendor of liturgical vestments, and pooled in the marble on the floor. The light made worshipers feel as if they were in the throne room of heaven.

In 1204, Crusaders attacked Constantinople and the Hagia

Sophia, leaving behind a legacy of bitterness against Western Christians that continues to this day. On May 29, 1453, the Ottoman Turks captured Constantinople and converted Hagia Sophia into a mosque. It remained a mosque until 1935, when it became a museum. Years later, the plaster used by the Muslims to cover the icons was removed, allowing today's visitors to view the original Christian artwork.

Icons

An icon is a religious image used as an aid to prayer. It might portray Christ, his mother Mary, an apostle, a saint, or an angel. It may be a painted panel or a mosaic. The worshiper does not worship the image, but instead uses the icon as an opening to prayer.

Icons were very popular by the sixth century, though certain segments of the population rejected them. One of the Ten Commandments states, "You shall not make yourself a carved image or any likeness of anything in heaven or on earth beneath or in the waters under the earth; you shall not bow down to them or serve them" (Exodus 20:4–5). After almost two-thirds of the empire's territory were lost during the Muslim expansion of the seventh century, eighth-century emperors Leo III and Constantine V interpreted the disaster as a punishment for the making of icons.

THE CRUSADERS PILLAGE CONSTANTINOPLE

Not since the world was made was there ever seen or won so great a treasure, or so noble or so rich, nor in the time of Alexander, nor in the time of Charlemagne, nor before, nor after, nor do I think myself that in the forty richest cities of the world had there been so much wealth as was found in Constantinople. For the Greeks say that two-thirds of the wealth of this world is in Constantinople and the other third scattered throughout the world.

—Robert of Clari, a French Crusader who witnessed
the Crusaders' pillage of Constantinople in 1204

For more than a century (726–842), icons were destroyed. This century was known as the period of *iconoclasm* ("breaking of images"). However, in the ninth century, there was a strong reaction against iconoclasm. The destruction of images was condemned as heresy. Restoration of images began in 843.

The making of icons was a liturgical art. They were designed to serve the highest of purposes: They taught divine truth (the sacred events of Scripture) without using words. Because of their sacred purpose, artists who fashioned icons had to follow exact precedents.

For example, it would not be proper to portray God the Father as an old man. According to Orthodox theology, God the Father has never been seen, and therefore, cannot be depicted in any kind of human form. Jesus, on the other hand, can be portrayed as a human being because he *was* human. The Holy Spirit should not be portrayed as a dove except in the case of the baptism of Jesus in the Jordan River, because that is the only time Scripture speaks of the Holy Spirit appearing in the form of a dove. Similarly, the Holy Spirit should be portrayed as tongues of fire only in depictions of Pentecost.

One of the most famous icons of Christ, housed at the Monastery of St. Catherine at Mount Sinai, dates back to the sixth century. In this image, Christ is dressed in the traditional royal purple tunic. He blesses the observer with his right hand, while his left hand holds the books of the Gospels. The eyes are slightly asymmetrical (one is bigger than the other), which draws attention to them. Some describe the face of Christ as tender and forgiving, while others see in it the soul-searching look of a judge. A halo surrounds Christ's head, symbolizing the divine light. Etched within the halo is the shape of a cross, plus the Greek words *ho on*, meaning "The One Who Is." This is the Greek version of the name of God as it was given to Moses.

In Orthodox Christianity, Mary is called *Theotokos* (literally, "the bearer" or "birthgiver" of God). The icon known as the *Virgin of Vladimir* was a gift brought from Constantinople to Russia in 1131. It is also called *Virgin Eleousa* ("Virgin of Tenderness"). In it, Mary holds the child Jesus in her right arm, and directs the observer's gaze to him with her left hand. The child clings tightly to his mother, and looks up at her face. Despite the closeness between them, the expression on Mary's face is pensive, slightly sad, as if she were looking into the future and seeing her son's death.

GOTHIC CATHEDRALS
Thirteenth-century Society

In the thirteenth century, European towns were growing rapidly. Their population included merchants and bankers. Construction was carried out by migrant bands of builders, masons, and "masters." Trade and craft guilds served to keep standards high, while also looking out for the interests of the occupation they represented.

The first European universities were established at the end of the twelfth century. (Until that time, monasteries had been the main educational centers.) The foremost center of learning in Europe was in Paris, France. The most prestigious of the faculties at the University of Paris was that of theology, and its greatest theologian was the Dominican monk Thomas Aquinas. Aquinas's philosophy remains the foundation of Roman Catholic thought to this day.

Reverence for Mary, the mother of Jesus, was evident in every area of life. In the thirteenth century, Western Christians composed songs dedicated to Mary, carried her image into battle on banners, and dedicated great cathedrals to her.

Chartres Cathedral is built over a crypt containing what is said to be the mantle of the Virgin Mary. Such keepsakes of the saints were known as relics. From one perspective, the sacred geography of medieval Europe was a map showing which churches and shrines housed the holy remains of which saints.

People went on pilgrimages to these sacred sites. The pilgrims were the predecessors of modern-day tourists but, while the pilgrims no doubt admired the beauty of landscapes and buildings, it was the connection with the sacred that interested them most. All of medieval Europe was on a journey toward God, and the holiness of the saints was both an example and an effective help on that journey.

Not all the saints were dead and buried. The Gothic period had its living saints as well. One of the most famous saints of all time was Francis of Assisi (1182–1226), who saw Christ not as a terrifying king or judge, but as a loving savior who walked among simple folk. Francis founded the religious order of monks known as the Franciscans. He wanted his monks to walk city streets preaching the gospel.

Obviously, the people who lived in thirteenth-century towns and cities were deeply religious. They put their growing economic resources into building cathedrals. The Gothic cathedrals that characterize this time period are some of the most impressive houses of worship the world has ever seen. Most are still standing today, and countless tourists visit them every year.

We do not know exactly how much of the economy of the time was devoted to the building of these churches, but it must have been a staggering percentage. In the twelfth and thirteenth centuries, more stone was quarried in France for the building of cathedrals than had been used in all the pyramids and other ancient monuments of Egypt.

The Cathedrals

The piety of the people, like the spires of their cathedrals, reached toward the heavens. The cathedrals drew people's gaze upward, away from the material world and its sensual labyrinth. The goal was union with God.

Unlike earlier cathedrals, Gothic interiors did not have massive walls. They were light and linear in appearance. Their great height was made possible by means of an external support system known as "flying buttresses." Like their cathedrals, medieval Christians sought to stand in God's presence, not on the basis of any internal strength or merit, but through the merits of Christ, the Virgin Mary, the saints, and the hierarchical body of believers that composed the medieval Church.

The medieval universe was organic and ordered, not individualistic. It was cooperative rather than competitive. Hopes soared and hearts leaped in anticipation of heaven, but heaven was not a competitive prize awarded on the basis of superior performance; it was a gift distributed through the downward flow of grace from Christ to the saints to ordinary believers.

As in the Hagia Sophia, in the Gothic cathedrals, light is a central element. Light floods down into the church through large windows that extend up into the highest recesses of the structure, so that the light, like God's grace, streams down from above. The long linear lines of the building and the light coming from above draw one's eyes up to the vaulted ceiling, between 80 and 144 feet high. The structure of the church directs the light down toward the people below, even as it directs the people's gaze upward to the light.

The altar of a Gothic cathedral stood on the east side, facing Jerusalem. Statues of saints and biblical events decorated the interior. Paintings and stained glass windows also contained scenes from Scripture or Church history. The visual art of the cathedrals taught the Bible to those who could not read. In the thirteenth century, that included most people.

These huge structures required many years to build, usually more than a century. Generations of artisans and financers were needed to complete a cathedral. Those who designed the building could not expect to see its finished form, and those who worshiped within it would never know the visionaries who began the work. It is almost impossible to imagine an undertaking of such immense proportions, not only in terms of physical size, but also in terms of the extent of the builders' faith.

Once completed, a cathedral served as the center of community life. The market was usually located nearby. Plays were performed on the steps. Cathedrals were the scene of coronations, investitures, and ordinations. Baptisms, confirmations, marriages, and funerals took place there, with burial of the dead on the church grounds. Of course, the most important event of all was the celebration of the Mass.

By the thirteenth century, the Mass was so filled with symbols and drama that the ordinary person could understand its spiritual meaning even without comprehending all of the Latin words spoken by the priest. Its high point was the moment of transubstantiation, when, through the words and actions of the celebrant, the bread and wine became the body and blood of Christ. Christ was then present in sacramental form in the midst of the congregation.

A short while later, communicants would individually receive Christ into their hearts and minds. This moment of intimate union with God took place within the vast space of a cathedral, which was the fruit of generations of labor. The immense and the immediate were joined. The cathedrals, like the God they glorified, were both vast and intimate, both awesome and sheltering.

PROTESTANT MUSIC

In those parts of Europe that became Protestant after the Reformation, statues in cathedrals were often destroyed and paintings whitewashed. The statues and paintings were believed to be contrary to the biblical injunction against the use of images in worship.

Protestants became great patronizers of the musical arts rather than the visual arts. In this section, we will look at some of the musical contributions of the Reformers and their spiritual descendants.

Music and theology alone are capable of giving peace and happiness to troubled souls. This plainly proves that the devil, the source of all unhappiness and worries, flees music as much as he does theology.

—Martin Luther

Martin Luther

Martin Luther (1483–1546), the first of the great sixteenth-century reformers, was thoroughly convinced of the value and power of music. "Next to the Word of God," he wrote, "the noble art of music is the greatest treasure in the world. It controls our thoughts, minds, hearts, and spirits. . . ." [20]

Luther stressed the importance of congregational participation in worship. To this end, he encouraged worship in the language of the people (the vernacular), as opposed to a sacred or traditional language like Greek or Latin. He also wrote hymns in the vernacular. These innovations helped increase congregational participation.

We have seen that the artwork in the Gothic cathedrals brought the teachings of the Bible to those who could not read. Music served that purpose in the Lutheran Church. Use of the vernacular meant that music could serve an educational purpose. Some of Luther's songs taught Lutheran theology. Others were Bible passages set to music.

DEAR CHRISTIANS, ONE AND ALL (verses 2 and 3)

by Martin Luther

Fast bound in Satan's chains I lay,
Death brooded darkly o'er me,
Sin was my torment night and day;
In sin my mother bore me.
But daily deeper still I fell;
My life became a living hell,
So firmly sin possessed me.

My own good works all came to naught,
No grace or merit gaining;
Free will against God's judgment fought,
Dead to all good remaining.
My fears increased till sheer despair
Left only death to be my share;
The pangs of hell I suffered.

Luther's theological emphasis on the salvation of the individual was accompanied by an interest in personal religious experience. The inner self, its struggles and torments as well as its joy and trust, appears in Lutheran theology, and also in Lutheran song. One example is "Dear Christians, One and All." Luther wrote the words to this song. In it, theological statements are interwoven with personal emotional expression.

Luther loved music. He grew up with it. All his life, he remembered how much his mother loved to sing. As a child, Luther was trained to become a *Kurrende* singer—that is, to be part of a chorus that sang at weddings and funerals.

Although the music Luther learned as a child was of the type beloved by peasants, his later education exposed him to the music of the great musicians of the Netherlands. By the time he was an adult, he had acquired considerable skill, not only as a singer, but also on the lute (a stringed instrument) and the "flute" (what we would call a recorder today).

Luther tapped a variety of sources for the nine hymnals that he put together. Melodies came from both German secular songs and Latin hymns. He wrote many of the words himself, and some of the melodies as well. His hymns are still sung today. Perhaps his best-known song is "A Mighty Fortress Is Our God."

Many people questioned the use of polyphony (voices singing separate parts) in church. Luther not only found polyphony acceptable, but he actually wrote songs with a four-part harmony similar to that found in secular music.

How strange and wonderful it is that one voice sings a simple unpretentious tune while three, four, or five other voices are also sung; these voices play and sway in joyful exuberance around the tune. . . . He must be a coarse clod and not worthy of hearing such charming music, who does not delight in this, and is not moved by such a marvel.

—Martin Luther

Although Luther was not opposed to the use of elaborate musical settings requiring highly skilled musicians and singers, he was of the firm opinion that the congregation should actively participate in at least some of the singing. The means of achieving this was chorales.

The chorale is the most distinctive and important Lutheran contribution to music. It is a congregational hymn in which the stanzas all use the same melody, making the song easier to sing. This is the most common type of song today, and it is used in secular as well as sacred settings. It was first fully developed in the Lutheran Church.

Many of Luther's hymns were in bar-form structure (AAB), in which the first line was repeated. This helped congregations to memorize them.

Although J. S. Bach made Lutheran organ music famous, Luther himself never used the organ to accompany hymns. He was not opposed to it because of its secular associations, as many were. Rather, he found it to be a "primitive" instrument because of its mean-tone tuning.[21]

Luther believed that the most intricate polyphonic musical forms should be sung in the churches, along with the simpler chorales. He was the only one who attempted to bring both sophisticated art music and folk melodies under a single roof.

The secular art music of the sixteenth century was too difficult for ordinary people to sing. The Calvinist tradition excluded art music entirely, using only simple psalms in its worship services. Lutherans, on the other hand, successfully encouraged and supported both sophisticated art music and simple congregational singing. The result was a musical tradition possessing richness, simplicity, and depth.

John Calvin

John Calvin agreed with Luther that worship, including songs, must be in a language that worshipers can understand. The two reformers were also bound by a common spirit of respect for the power of music. In his *Preface to the Psalter*, Calvin wrote, "There is scarcely in the world anything which is more able to turn or bend this way and that the morals of men."[22] When words are accompanied by a melody, they penetrate the heart more deeply:

> It is true that every bad word (as St. Paul has said) perverts good manner, but when the melody is with it, it pierces the heart more strongly, and enters into it; in a like manner as through a funnel, the wine is poured into the vessel; so also the venom and the corruption is distilled to the depths of the heart by the melody. A good song, on the other hand, can inflame the hearts of men to invoke and praise God with a more vehement and ardent zeal.[23]

Calvin and Luther parted ways, however, over the adaptation of secular melodies for church use. Calvin thought that church music should be recognizably distinct from secular songs. One must not sound like the other. Church music needed to have weight and majesty. It should never be light or frivolous.

Calvin's Puritan and Presbyterian theological descendants adopted the "regulative principle of worship" as found in the *Westminster Confession of Faith*. The regulative principle stated that pure and acceptable worship must be prescribed by God himself—it must be commanded in the Bible. It was not enough that there be nothing in Scripture prohibiting it; there had to be positive support for the practice in Scripture. On the basis of this principle, these Protestants removed all instrumental music and organs from their churches, just as they removed or whitewashed all statues and paintings. One was as sure a sign of corruption as the other.

One might object that the Bible makes plentiful references to praising God with the accompaniment of wind and stringed instruments. David himself played the harp. In Calvin's view, however, these things were part of an earlier dispensation that, like the Jerusalem Temple in which they were used, was abolished with the coming of Christ:

> The Levites, under the law, were justified in making use of instrumental music in the worship of God; it having been his will to train his people, while they were yet tender and like children, by such rudiments until the coming of Christ. But now, when the clear light of the gospel has dissipated the shadows of the law and taught us that God is to be served in a simpler form, it would be to act a foolish and mistaken part to imitate that which the prophet enjoined only upon those of his own time.[24]

The Catholic Church, which did allow organs in churches (but not until the thirteenth century), was accused of having a "Judaizing hermeneutic (method of interpretation)." The fact that Catholics had retained other practices found in ancient Israel (including priests and an altar on which a sacrifice was offered) lent fuel to the polemic.

Those Protestants who did not agree with Calvin, and chose to use organs and other musical instruments in their churches, were accused of "will-worship"—in other words, worshiping according to human will rather than God's will.[25] For the seventeenth-century descendants of Calvin who removed organs from churches, it was a matter of "proclaiming the sovereignty of God in worship and over every area of life."[26]

Charles Wesley

In the eighteenth century, when most people traveled on horseback, it was said that you could tell that a Methodist was coming by his singing. Methodists had a lot of material to choose from: Charles Wesley was one of Christianity's most prolific hymn writers.

John and Charles Wesley were the founders of the organization that evolved into the Methodist Church. They were brothers. John was older; he was the better-known preacher and organizer. Charles was Methodism's poet and hymn writer.

Charles Wesley may well be the greatest hymn writer that Christianity has ever known. He composed approximately six thousand hymns, many of them still in common use today. Wesley wrote such favorites as "Come Thou Long Expected Jesus" (sung during Advent), "Hark the Herald Angels Sing" (sung at Christmas), "Christ the Lord Is Risen Today" (sung at Easter), and "Love Divine, All Loves Excelling."

Wesley's hymns are known for their theological soundness and evangelistic message. His songs were used to educate people in proper doctrine.

Wesley's hymns appeal to the emotions as well as the intellect, however. They have retained their popularity for so long largely because of their emphasis on personal spiritual experience.

Charles and John Wesley together produced some sixty hymnals. The most definitive of these was the 1780 version. Its 525 songs contained the entire spiritual message of John Wesley

LOVE DIVINE, ALL LOVES EXCELLING (first two verses)

by Charles Wesley

Love divine, all loves excelling,
Joy of heav'n, to earth come down!
Fix in us thy humble dwelling,
All thy faithful mercies crown.
Jesus, thou art all compassion,
Pure, unbounded love thou art;
Visit us with thy salvation,
Enter ev'ry trembling heart.

Breathe, oh, breathe thy loving Spirit
Into ev'ry troubled breast;
Let us all in thee inherit;
Let us find thy promised rest.
Take away the love of sinning;
Alpha and Omega be;
End of faith, as its beginning,
Set our hearts at liberty.

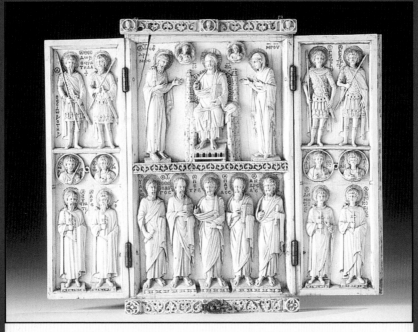

Harbaville Triptych: Deesis and Saints. This Byzantine triptych, or carving with three side-by-side parts, is from tenth-century Constantinople. Its middle panel depicts Jesus on a throne, surrounded by John the Baptist and the Virgin Mary, while the surrounding panels are filled with apostles, saints, bishops, and martyrs in prayer. Carved out of ivory with traces of gold leaf, this important example of Byzantine classicism demonstrates a rebirth of the ornamental arts.

A relief is a type of sculpture in which a form projects from a background. This Byzantine relief uses silver and depicts the Virgin Mary with her child, Jesus. Mary and Jesus are common subjects of religious art because of their central role in Christianity.

Hagia Sophia: Emperor Justinian commissioned the great domed church Hagia Sophia, meaning "holy wisdom," to be built in Constantinople (present-day Istanbul, Turkey). Constructed between 532 and 537, the massive structure is 270 feet by 240 feet, and its dome, representing the vault of heaven, sits 200 feet above the floor on four massive pillars. When the Ottoman Turks captured Constantinople in 1453, they converted the Hagia Sophia into a mosque, which accounts for the Islamic structures, such as minarets, seen on the building's exterior.

An icon is any picture or sculpture regarded as an object of veneration, acting as a connection between the human and the divine. Icons are not meant to be worshiped, but rather to help teach divine truth and act as an opening to prayer. Though some Christians rejected icons as a violation of the commandment forbidding the making of images, most considered the making of icons a liturgical art. This 1640 Russian icon depicts the crucifixion of Christ.

Located in St. Catherine Monastery, Mount Sinai, Egypt, this twelfth-century icon illustrates instructions given to monks by sixth-century abbot Johannes Klimax. Good monks climb up the heavenly ladder to perfection, while black devils drag bad monks down to hell. St. Catherine's was commissioned by Emperor Justinian in the mid-sixth century, and now houses a vast collection of priceless art.

This fifth-century bronze monogrammatic cross found in Monastero, Italy, is an important example of early Christian cultic symbolism. The Greek letter "P" on the top changes it from a Latin cross to a Christogram, while the Alpha and Omega represent Jesus's words in the New Testament, "I am the Alpha and the Omega . . . the Beginning and the End."

This twelfth-century mosaic located in the Cathedral of Cefalu in Sicily depicts Christ Pantocrator, or Master of All Creation, holding his right hand out in blessing and displaying Greek and Latin texts in his left. Mosaic was the main decoration for Byzantine and early Christian churches up until the fifteenth century when it was widely replaced by fresco. This beautiful but laborious technique required the artist to create a design by setting tiny pieces of colored glass or stone in plaster.

Mosaics were so prevalent that they sometimes were even used for floors, as in this sixth-century example from St. John's Church in Gerasa, Jordan. This mosaic depicts Alexandria, Egypt, one of the most important cities of the time and an early center of Christianity.

Paintings of the saints fill the Tomb of King Marian, shown here, at the Church of Samtravo in Mtskheta, Georgia, built in the eleventh century. King Marian III converted to Christianity around A.D. 330 and made Georgia one of the first countries to adopt Christianity as its official state religion.

as delivered to the thousands who heard his sermons and read his writings. It was through Charles's music that most believers learned Methodist theology.

AFRICAN-AMERICAN SPIRITUALS

African-American spirituals were songs sung by slaves as they worked and worshiped on Southern plantations in the United States. About five thousand spirituals have been preserved. Almost all of them are anonymous, meaning that we don't know who composed them.

African-American spirituals have influenced history and culture both nationally and internationally. They were the antecedents of such popular musical forms as gospel, blues, rock and roll, jazz, and hip-hop.

Spirituals had many levels of meaning: political, personal, and spiritual. Prior to the Civil War (1861–1865), some spirituals contained a kind of code that referred to the Underground Railroad, an organization that helped slaves escape to free territory in the Northern states or Canada. To conceal what they were

NOBODY KNOWS DE TROUBLE I'VE SEEN

Nobody knows de trouble I've seen,
Nobody knows but Jesus.
Nobody knows de trouble I've seen, Glory hallelujah!
Sometimes I'm up, sometimes I'm down
Oh yes, Lord! Sometimes I'm almos' to de groun';
Oh yes, Lord! Oh nobody knows de trouble I've seen,
Nobody knows but Jesus.
Nobody knows de trouble I've seen, Glory hallelujah!
If you get there before I do,
Oh yes, Lord! Tell all my friends I'm coming too,
Oh yes, Lord! Oh nobody knows de trouble I've seen,
Nobody knows but Jesus.
Nobody knows de trouble I've seen, Glory hallelujah.

—Arranged by H. T. Burleigh

talking about from their masters, slaves called the North "my home" or "Sweet Canaan, the Promised Land." They called the Ohio River, which marked a major boundary between the North and the South "Jordan." Often, runaway slaves would walk in the water, so that dogs could not follow their tracks. As they got closer to free territory, they would be hidden in a carriage, and there they would ride to freedom. Spirituals like "The Gospel Train" (a name for the Underground Railroad), "Wade in the Water," and "Swing Low, Sweet Chariot" kept alive a hope for an end to slavery.

Spirituals were not popular right after the Civil War. Most African Americans did not want to remember the hard days of slavery. The songs resurfaced in the late nineteenth century, and have remained a part of popular culture ever since. Henry Thacker (H. T.) Burleigh (1866–1949) composed and performed many of the spirituals that have come down to us. Czech composer Antonin Dvorak met Burleigh when the latter was a student at the National Conservatory of Music. It was from Burleigh that Dvorak first heard "Swing Low, Sweet Chariot." Dvorak's Symphony No. 9 uses parts of this spiritual.

At the time Burleigh was arranging spirituals, their personal and spiritual interpretations were primary. Emancipation had brought an end to slavery, but not to oppression. "Nobody Knows de Trouble I've Seen," arranged by Burleigh, gives voice to the

DEEP RIVER

Deep river, my home is over Jordan,
Deep river, Lord, I want to cross over into camp-ground.
Deep river, my home is over Jordan
Deep river, Lord, I want to cross over into camp-ground.
Oh, don't you want to go to that gospel feast,
That promised land where all is peace?
Oh deep river, Lord, I want to cross over into camp-ground.

—Arranged by H. T. Burleigh

experience of oppression. The lyrics combine a graphic realism about the emotions accompanying oppression with a sense of the close presence of Jesus, and a strong hope that suffering will not be permanent. The singer believes in a heaven in which he or she will be reunited with loved ones and their troubles will be gone.

As the decades rolled by, and equal opportunity was nowhere to be found, many African Americans began to think that there might not be any freedom from suffering in this world. This resulted in a great yearning to "cross over Jordan" (the river now serving as a symbol for a troubled life) and enter the "campground" (heaven, the promised land), as masterfully expressed in Burleigh's "Deep River."

As a final example of the combination of the personal and spiritual meanings found in many African-American spirituals, consider "Sometimes I Feel Like a Motherless Child." Many slave children were sold away from their families at an early age, some so young that they had no memories of their mother's faces. They did not know when or where they were born. They had no birthday to celebrate, and no family to celebrate with. That is what it means to be "a motherless chile (child)." As a people, the slaves were "a long ways from home," because they had been taken away from western Africa. As individuals, they were also "a long ways from home," because they were often sold to someone living in a faraway state. Since they were not allowed to read or write, they could not keep in contact with friends and relatives. Finally, the slaves were "a long ways from

SOMETIMES I FEEL LIKE A MOTHERLESS CHILD

Sometimes I feel like a motherless chile,
Sometimes I feel like a motherless chile,
Sometimes I feel like a motherless chile,
A long ways from home
A long ways from home . . .

—Arranged by H. T. Burleigh

home" because "home" was a metaphor for heaven, and living in slavery was certainly "a long ways" from paradise.

EVANGELICAL REFORMERS
IN NINETEENTH-CENTURY AMERICA

As the previous section demonstrates, one does not have to be famous, powerful, or wealthy to make a difference. The anonymous African Americans who created the spirituals changed the course of history, of music, and of Christianity. African-American spirituals were the product not of famous individual artists, but of a lot of ordinary people. The culture of ordinary people is called popular culture. In this section, we will continue our consideration of popular culture.

In the nineteenth century, American evangelicals sent missionaries overseas and worked for moral reform in the United States. Women played a large role in both endeavors.

Woman's Christian Temperance Union (WCTU)

In the late nineteenth and early twentieth centuries, the Woman's Christian Temperance Union was the largest women's organization in both the United States and the world. As WCTU used the term, *temperance* meant abstaining from alcohol. WCTU succeeded in changing American culture and the position of women within it.

In the nineteenth century, liquor consumption was at an all-time high in the United States. Alcohol was the third most important industrial product in 1810, accounting for nearly 10 percent of the total national manufacturing output. By 1840, consumption of alcohol was approximately three times what it would be in 1940.[27]

Liquor was more readily available than water, which was scarce in many urban areas. It was less expensive than milk. Furthermore, both water and milk carried diseases. Despite its relatively low price, Americans spent over $1 billion on alcohol in 1900. In that same year, only $900 million was spent on meat, $150 million was donated to churches, and less than $200 million was spent on public education.

Women were not allowed in saloons, but temperance was a women's issue. Men who were drunk often beat their wives, neglected their children, and failed miserably as economic providers for their families. Nonetheless, in 1900, a woman possessed no rights to her children in thirty-seven states (out of forty-five states at that time). The children belonged to the husband alone. In addition, a woman's possessions and earnings were her husband's property. If he wanted to squander them on liquor, he was legally able to do so.

Recognizing that they had been rendered powerless in their own homes, women took to the streets. In 1873, Protestant evangelical women started a "praying-in-saloons" crusade. Despite the movement's name, these women usually did not enter the saloons. Rather, they stood on the curb in front of saloons and sang Christian hymns.

These crusades spread across the country, revolutionizing women's place in the public domain. Most demonstrations were nonviolent, but in some instances, dogs were set on the women, or mobs of brewers rushed at them with bats.

When all was said and done, the fruits of the temperance movement's labors—Prohibition (a legal ban on alcohol production and consumption that went into effect in 1920)—was not a success. The amendment was repealed in 1933. On the other hand, after Prohibition, Americans consumed less alcohol, and alcohol was no longer considered a necessity of life. It is now one of a small number of items subject to a "sin tax," which indicates its fall from respectability. Equally important was the fact that the antiliquor crusades provided evidence that granting women a role in public life could be beneficial to the nation.

Harriet Beecher Stowe: *Uncle Tom's Cabin*

Writing was one of the few avenues by which women could influence public opinion in the nineteenth century. Harriet Beecher Stowe's novel *Uncle Tom's Cabin* drew attention to the evil of slavery by showing its impact on families. Husbands and wives, parents and children, could be sold apart much as one might sell the pieces of a set of furniture separately.

Tom, the character for whom the book is named, is a slave. Ironically, he is in many ways freer than anyone else. He obeys his masters, but he fears only God. The cruel Simon Legree, Tom's final master, hates Tom for his inner freedom. Tom will not grovel, but he will bear any load. He serves freely, not because he is a slave but because he is a Christian. This finally drives Legree into such a rage that he beats Tom to death.

Eliza, another character in *Uncle Tom's Cabin*, is the mother of five-year-old Harry. Like Tom, Eliza believes that she must "obey master and mistress" in order to be a Christian. Arthur Shelby owns Eliza and Harry. He is a kind man, but when he falls into debt, he sells little Harry to a slave trader. Overhearing the transaction and knowing that her son is about to be taken from her, Eliza flees with Harry, breaking the law.

The Ohio River was the boundary between the slave state of Kentucky and the free state of Ohio. When Eliza reaches the river, it is swollen and turbulent with great cakes of floating ice. There was no ferry, so Eliza, pursued by slave catchers and clutching Harry, jumps from one sheet of ice to another until she reaches the Ohio shore.

Uncle Tom's Cabin required readers to wrestle with God's law versus secular law. It also required them to sort through opposing views of what the Bible says about slavery. The book presented an argument that true Christians could not condone slavery.

Harriet Beecher Stowe's passionate portrayal of the lives of slaves galvanized antislavery sentiment in the United States. When Stowe met President Abraham Lincoln in 1862, he greeted her by saying, "So you are the little woman who wrote the book that started this great war [the Civil War]!" [28]

Sojourner Truth

On a dark night in 1844, a camp meeting was held in Northampton, Massachusetts. Strong emotions were not rare in Bible camps, but the fear that held this meeting in its grasp was an unholy fear.

About a hundred wild young men had invaded the camp. When confronted by camp leaders, the mob threatened to burn the tents.

A woman in her late forties hid behind a trunk in a back corner of one of the tents. She feared for her life. She was the only black person in the camp; that alone might make her a target.

"Shall I run away and hide from the devil?" she asked herself. "Me, a servant of the living God? Have I not faith enough to go out and quell that mob, when I know it is written, 'One shall chase a thousand'?"

While the preacher trembled at this pulpit, the woman strode through the din and confusion to the top of a small rise of ground. She began to sing in a powerful voice about the resurrection of Christ.

The young men rushed toward her. She paused, then spoke in a gentle but firm tone, saying, "Why do you come about me with clubs and sticks? I am not doing harm to anyone."

"We're not going to hurt you, old woman," said a voice. This was quickly followed by a chorus: "Sing to us, old woman!"

She preached and sang to her strange flock for several hours, allowing the preacher to work unmolested. When the meeting was over, the young men policed their own, and everyone left the camp without mishap.

This was not the first time that the brave Sojourner Truth had accomplished the seemingly impossible. In 1828, with slavery still fully legal in the South, she strode the streets of Alabama, barefoot and dusty, with no money, determined to find and take back her young son, who had been sold there.

She talked to dozens of people who didn't want to listen until she found a lawyer to prosecute her case. She became the first black woman ever to win a court case against a white man.

When she was in her thirties, Truth had a vision of God's glory. "Oh, God!" she exclaimed, "I did not know you were so big!" She was ashamed that she had addressed God as if the Almighty were an ordinary being like herself.

She wished she had someone to stand between herself and God, whom she believed she had insulted. At length, a "friend" appeared, but she did not know who he was.

"Who are you?" she asked. To her surprise, the figure answered, "It is Jesus." She had heard of Jesus before, but had formed the impression that he was an eminent man, not a divine figure. The experience dramatically changed her life as a Christian.

After being freed from slavery in 1827, Truth worked as a domestic servant in New York. In 1843, she began to travel and preach. She eventually became a famous abolitionist and suffragist.

In 1851, in Akron, Ohio, several male ministers attacked the resolutions under discussion at a women's rights convention. One claimed greater rights and privileges for men on the basis of women's need for help, another because of the supposedly superior male intellect, and a third because of the "manhood of Christ." A fourth decried the "sin of our first mother [Eve]."

As Sojourner Truth rose from her seat in the corner, her lanky six-foot frame towered over most of those present. The former slave retorted that no man had ever helped her into a carriage or over a mud puddle. Not one had ever given up his seat for her.

The size of one's intellect, Truth said, had nothing to do with rights for black people or for women. People have rights because they're human, not because they are smart.

Addressing the claim that women have fewer rights than men because Christ was a man, she exclaimed, "Where did your Christ come from? . . . From God and a woman! Man had nothing to do with him."

As for "Mother Eve," if she was strong enough to turn the world upside down on her own, Truth said, all the women at that convention working together ought to be able to get it back upright. And, since they were willing, the men had better let them do that!

Once, Truth attended a speech by famed abolitionist Frederick Douglass. After describing the many wrongs suffered by African

Americans, Douglass concluded that whites would never agree to justice. He argued that black people must fight for it with the strength of their own arms.

In the hush that followed, Truth's deep voice could be heard throughout the house. "Frederick," she asked, "IS GOD DEAD?" Instantly, the call to arms became a call to faith.

Douglass himself described Truth as "a strange compound of wit and wisdom, of wild enthusiasm and flintlike common sense."[29] She demonstrated clearly what strength of character combined with a devout belief in Christianity could accomplish.

8

Calendar
and Holidays

And when He had taken some bread and given thanks,
He broke it, and gave it to them, saying,
"This is My body which is given for you;
do this in remembrance of Me."

—Luke 22:19

CALENDARS

Today, the Gregorian (Western) Christian calendar is used internationally, although many cultures continue to use their own calendars for regional or local matters. There are approximately forty calendars currently in use in various places around the world. We also know about a number of calendars, such as the Roman and Mayan calendars, that are no longer used. The Gregorian calendar had its origins in a pre-Christian Roman calendar. In order to understand what it is that makes the Christian calendar unique, we have to be aware of the variety found in calendars.

Solar and Lunar Calendars

The main problem for calendar makers has always been how to establish a single recurrent pattern involving both sun and moon movements. Because there is no simple way to do this, most calendars follow either the sun or the moon cycles, but not both.

The Gregorian calendar is a solar calendar. So is its predecessor, the Julian calendar, which is still used by most Eastern Christians. Like all solar calendars, the Christian calendars follow the movements of the sun fairly accurately. Because the movements of the sun with respect to Earth are what create the seasons of the year, the seasons will appear to be fixed with respect to a solar calendar—that is, they will always come at the same time of the year. The weakness of a solar calendar is that it tells little about the movements of the moon. The "months" (literally, "moons") on a solar calendar have only a vague correlation with the phases of the moon.

A lunar calendar has the opposite set of strengths and weaknesses. It tracks the movements of the moon, but gives little or no information about seasonal variations due to solar motion. Consequently, a given month can occur in any season of the year. If the Gregorian calendar were a lunar calendar, January would not always come in winter. Sometimes it would come in winter, but other times in fall, summer, or spring. The lunar calendar that is most widely used today is the Islamic calendar.

Some calendars do attempt to track both sun and moon movements. This means that the first day of each month should fall on or near a new moon, and, in addition, a given month will remain in the same season of the year. The months of such a calendar will line up with the lunar phases and the years will line up with the solar seasons, both at the same time. This accomplishment necessitates some fairly complex calendar rules.

The Hebrew calendar is an example of a calendar that tracks both the sun and the moon. An ordinary year on the Hebrew calendar has twelve months, but a "leap" year has an entire extra month inserted in the middle of the year, making a thirteen-month leap year. Seven such extra months are inserted in a nineteen-year cycle. The result is that there are 235 months every nineteen years. It so happens that 235 months is very close to nineteen solar years, allowing the Hebrew calendar to match both moon and sun cycles quite nicely.

No calendar is a simple matter. That is why, in ancient times, the priests were in charge of the calendar. The priests were the most highly educated members of society. Predicting the most auspicious date for planting, or the appropriate date for a prescribed sacrifice to the gods, was a tricky—and very serious—matter; getting it wrong could actually result in the priest's execution.

Where Did the Christian Calendar Come From?

The earliest Christians lived in the Roman Empire. They used the Julian calendar introduced by Julius Caesar in 45 B.C. The first change made by Christians occurred in the sixth century, when a monk named Dionysius Exiguus attempted to change the year "1" to the year of Christ's birth. Previously, the calendar had begun with the year of the founding of Rome (753 B.C.).

Dionysius made a mistake. He fixed Jesus's birth on December 25, 753 A.U.C. (*ab urbe condita*; in other words, since the founding of Rome). However, the New Testament records that Jesus was born during the reign of Herod the Great (Matthew 2), who died in 750 A.U.C. If the New Testament is historically accurate on this point, Jesus could have been born no later than the year of Herod's death. Since Matthew states that Herod ordered the slaying of all children two years old or younger, Jesus's birth probably took place at least a year or two prior to that. The Christian calendar was never restarted to correct Dionysius's error. Christians just live with the fact that Jesus was born sometime between 4 and 6 B.C., or perhaps earlier.

The Julian calendar was in common use until Pope Gregory XIII, in accordance with instructions from the Council of Trent (1545–1563), introduced the Gregorian calendar in 1582. The Julian calendar estimated a year as 365¼ days, resulting in an error of one day in approximately 128 years. By the sixteenth century, the error was obvious with respect to the seasons of the year. Hence, a correction was made that resulted in the Gregorian calendar.

Most Orthodox churches continue to use the Julian calendar. For that reason, Easter often comes up to several weeks later among Eastern Christians than it does among Western Christians.

THE CHRISTIAN YEAR
The Christian calendar keeps track of Christian holidays and feast days. In general, the more traditional and liturgical the church, the more observances it is likely to have. Almost all Christian groups observe Easter and Christmas. Orthodox, Catholics, and Anglicans also observe the feast days of Mary and other saints.

Easter
Easter has always been the most important Christian holiday. It celebrates the resurrection of Jesus.

Easter was originally called the "Christian Passover," because the first Christians celebrated it as the Jewish Passover with an additional Christian layer of meaning. The Jewish Passover commemorates the process of freeing the Hebrews from slavery in Egypt. The Christian Passover continued to celebrate that event, but also used the day to remember Jesus's death and rising in freedom from the grave three days later.

The Jewish Passover is a lunar festival. Its descendant, Easter, remains a movable feast connected to the full moon. This means that Easter is not celebrated on the same day every year. The Western Church (both Protestant and Catholic) celebrates Easter on the first Sunday after the full moon that follows the spring equinox (the spring equinox occurs on or near March 21). Consequently, Easter is celebrated by Western Christians either in late March or sometime in April.

THE COPTIC CHRISTIAN CALENDAR OF EGYPT

Not all Christians use either the Gregorian or the Julian calendar. The Christians of Egypt, for example, have their own calendar. The Christians of Egypt are called "Copts." They make up approximately 10 percent of Egypt's population.

The Coptic Church is one of the most ancient Christian churches in the world. It claims to hold an unbroken line of patriarchal succession extending back to the Apostle Mark. According to Church historian Eusebius, Mark came to Egypt sometime between A.D. 41 and 44, and visited the country again between 61 and 68.

The Coptic Christian Orthodox Church of Egypt has contributed much to the Christian world. Monasticism was born in Egypt. The Coptic Church is also known for its reverence for the martyrs. It has contributed to their ranks, for it is a church that has frequently suffered persecution.

Copts fast for over 210 days out of the 365 days in the year, more than any other Christian group. Fasting means they consume no animal products (including meat, poultry, fish, milk, eggs, and butter). In addition, a Copt may not eat or drink anything at all between sunrise and sunset on fast days.

The current Coptic patriarch, Pope Shenouda III, is the 117th patriarch to occupy the chair of St. Mark in the See of Alexandria. The Coptic Church today is a strong supporter of the ecumenical

At first, Easter was a one-day festival commemorating both the death and the resurrection of Jesus. However, as pilgrimages to Jerusalem grew in popularity, and pilgrims retraced Jesus's steps during the final week of his life, auxiliary holidays grew up. The Sunday before Easter is "Palm Sunday;" it commemorates Jesus's triumphal entry into Jerusalem. He rode into Jerusalem on a donkey and was hailed as a king. People threw palm branches on the ground in front of him, symbolically granting him royal status. In many countries, this day is celebrated with a public procession.

The Thursday before Easter is called "Maundy Thursday." It commemorates Jesus's last meal with his disciples before he was killed. Jehovah's Witnesses call this day the "Memorial of Christ's

movement. It was a founding member of the World Council of Churches. It also conducts dialogues aimed at resolving the theological differences that separate the Orthodox, Catholic, Presbyterian, and evangelical branches of Christianity.

The date that marks the Coptic New Year has its roots in the time of the Egyptian pharaohs. The appearance of the Dog Star (Sothis) signaled the rise of the Nile River, which flooded the surrounding plains and prepared the fields for planting to begin. Because this date marked the beginning of a new growing season, it became New Year's Day. Coptic Christianity adopted this date for the New Year, but it established the inaugural year of its calendar on the basis of third-century events.

The Christian Church in Egypt suffered intense persecution during the reign of Roman Emperor Diocletian. Diocletian ordered the demolition of all churches and the burning of the Scriptures. Thousands of people were tortured and martyred. So many Christians lost their lives during this period that the Coptic Church dates its calendar from 284, the year of Diocletian's accession to the throne. That year marked the beginning of the Era of Martyrs. Whereas in the Gregorian calendar dates carry the initials "A.D." (*anno domini*, or "the year of our Lord"), in the Coptic calendar they are initialed "A.M." (*anno martyri*, or "the year of the martyrs").

Death." It is their one and only religious holiday of the year. The Friday before Easter is "Good Friday;" it is the day when Jesus died on the cross. The entire week before Easter is known as "Holy Week."

Another tradition that grew up around Easter involved those preparing for baptism. In the Western Church, it became the custom to prepare new Christians for baptism during the forty

THE ORTHODOX CHRISTIAN YEAR

One of the most complex of the Christian calendars is that of the Orthodox churches. The Orthodox New Year is September 1, not January 1. The Orthodox year is an alternation of feasts and fasts.

FEASTS
The most significant feast is Pascha (Easter), which is known as the Feast of Feasts. Next in importance are the Twelve Great Feasts:

- The Nativity of the Mother of God (September 8)

- The Exaltation of the Honorable and Life-giving Cross (September 14)

- The Presentation of the Mother of God in the Temple (November 21)

- The Nativity of Christ (Christmas) (December 25)

- The Epiphany (January 6)

- The Presentation of Our Lord in the Temple (February 2)

- The Annunciation of the Mother of God (March 25)

- The Entry of Our Lord into Jerusalem (Palm Sunday) (one week before Pascha)

- The Ascension of Our Lord Jesus Christ (forty days after Pascha)

- Pentecost (Trinity Sunday) (fifty days after Pascha)

days of Lent, and to officially welcome them into the Church during the Easter Vigil. (In the Eastern Church, baptism takes place on the Epiphany, on January 6.)

Lent is a forty-day period of repentance and fasting that precedes Easter. It begins on Ash Wednesday. In some churches, people receive ashes on their forehead on Ash Wednesday, to remind them that they will one day die and have to meet their

- The Transfiguration of Our Savior Jesus Christ (August 6)

- The Dormition (Falling Asleep) of the Mother of God (August 15)

In addition to the Twelve Great Feasts, there are many more feast days that commemorate events in the life of Christ, the Virgin Mary, or a saint.

FASTS
There are four main fasts:

- The Great Fast (Lent)—begins on a Monday seven weeks before Pascha

- The Fast of the Apostles—starts on the Monday eight days after Pentecost, and ends on the Feast of Saints Peter and Paul on June 28 (it may last between one and six weeks)

- The Dormition Fast—August 1 to August 14 (lasts two weeks)

- The Christmas Fast—lasts forty days, from November 15 to December 24

Orthodox Christians also observe a number of one-day fasts that take place on or just prior to feast days. In addition, all Wednesdays and Fridays except those that fall between Christmas and Epiphany, during Easter week, and during the week after Pentecost, are fast days.

During the Lenten fast, meat, fish, and all animal foods (including lard, eggs, and dairy products) are forbidden. Wine and oil are also prohibited during Lent.

maker. In the Roman Catholic Church, as the priest sketches an ashen cross on each person's forehead, he says, "Remember, mortal, you are dust, and to dust you will return."[30]

Christmas

The other major Christian holiday, Christmas, also has a period of repentance that precedes it. The pre-Christmas period is known as Advent ("approach") because it is the time in which the birth of the Messiah is drawing near.

Christmas commemorates the birth of Jesus. It is a fixed feast, celebrated every year on December 25. No one knows the actual date of Jesus's birth. December 25 was chosen by Julius I, bishop of Rome, in A.D. 350.

Christmas is Christianity's most popular holiday, and its most contested. Despite the fact that more Christians go to church on this day than any other, Christmas is often criticized for having become too secularized. This is nothing new. Christmas has been involved in a tug of war between its Christian and non-Christian elements for almost two thousand years.

At first, Christmas was celebrated with a special church service, and nothing more. It lacked the elements of fun and social celebration that are associated with it today. Epiphany (January 6) was more popular than Christmas. Gifts were given on Epiphany, not Christmas, because Epiphany commemorated the Wise Men's presentation of their gifts to the infant Jesus. Christmas was quiet and solemn. It would grow in popularity only after absorbing elements from non-Christian celebrations.

By far, the largest non-Christian contributors to Christmas were the winter solstice celebrations that took place in Rome and in northern Europe. The winter solstice, the shortest day of the year (usually December 21 or 22), is also the beginning of the lengthening hours of daylight that culminate in new life in the spring. Solstice festivals celebrate the return of light and life.

The Roman Saturnalia began in mid-December and continued for weeks. It featured halls decked with laurel garlands, feasting, visiting friends, and gift giving.

In northern Europe, December's end was a perfect time for a celebration. Livestock was slaughtered so the animals would not to have to be fed through the winter. Wine and beer had finished fermenting and were ready for consumption.

The farther north one went in Europe, the more marked was the sun's waning as winter approached. In some parts of Scandinavia, the sun disappeared for many days. When scouts reported the first signs of the sun's return, large Yule logs were set on fire. The feasting lasted for as long as the logs burned, sometimes for up to twelve days.

Over the course of centuries, Christians appropriated the solstice's emphasis on light and life. By the late Middle Ages, Christmas had become a season of good cheer. It included Yule logs, evergreen decorations, and gift giving.

By the fourteenth and fifteenth centuries, Christmas had won its competition with the pagan holidays by becoming more "merry" than they were. However, this success would soon be challenged. Some sixteenth-century reformers expressed concern about the nonbiblical elements of popular Christmas celebrations. These concerns peaked in mid-seventeenth-century England, with the rise of the Puritans.

The English Civil War, which began in 1642, pitted the Puritans and Parliament against the Anglican Church and the king. Following the execution of the archbishop of Canterbury and the king, Oliver Cromwell assumed leadership of the newly formed Commonwealth (1649–1660). He imposed social and religious laws favored by the Puritans. As part of their effort to rid England of decadence, the Puritans canceled Christmas.

Cromwell turned out to be a tyrant. His unpopular measures, including the elimination of Christmas, were rescinded in 1660 when the Commonwealth dissolved and the monarchy was restored.

The Puritans, having lost the war, fled in large numbers to America, especially to the northern colonies. There, Christmas was not celebrated. In 1659, the General Court of Massachusetts enacted a law making any observance of December 25 (other than going to church) an offense punishable by law. Until 1681, anyone found exhibiting the Christmas spirit in Boston was fined five shillings.

On the other hand, many of the southern colonies, where the Anglican Church was dominant, celebrated Christmas. In colonial Virginia, Christmas included church attendance, dinner, dancing, evergreen decorations, and visiting with family and friends. After the American Revolution, English customs, including Christmas, fell out of favor. Congress was in session on December 25, 1789, the first Christmas after the adoption of the new constitution. The United States would not embrace Christmas until well into the nineteenth century; it was not declared a federal holiday until 1870.

Nineteenth-century America was responsible for making Christmas a holiday that centered on children. Until that time, Christmas celebrations had been directed solely toward adults. It was German, Irish, and Dutch immigrants who brought the customs that enabled Americans to convert Christmas into a family-centered holiday.

While Americans of Puritan persuasion avoided Christmas trees, seeing them as pagan symbols, Pennsylvania German settlements enjoyed them. In the nineteenth century, a large influx of German and Irish immigrants undermined the Puritan sensibilities of much of the country, and the United States embraced the Christmas tree.

Nineteenth-century America also rediscovered St. Nicholas, a third- to fourth-century monk and bishop known for his piety and gift giving. Although most Christian saints did not remain popular in Protestant lands after the Reformation, St. Nicholas kept his influence among Dutch Protestants. Immigrants from Holland brought their December 6 celebration of "Sinter Klaas" (*Sinter Klaas* is short for "Sint Nikolaas") to the United States. Americans secularized the saint; Santa Claus had no association with piety and saintliness.

Other Holidays

In addition to the holidays of the Easter and Christmas seasons, many Christians celebrate Ascension and Pentecost. Ascension is observed forty days after Easter. It commemorates the day on which Jesus was taken up into heaven, leaving Earth after he had appeared to a number of his followers after his resurrection.

Pentecost is celebrated on the seventh Sunday after Easter. It was a Jewish festival before it became a Christian holiday. As the disciples were celebrating the Jewish festival of Pentecost, the Holy Spirit descended upon them in tongues of fire (Acts 2). They were empowered with the gifts of the Spirit, including speaking in tongues and the ability to heal people. Pentecost is also considered the birthday of the Christian Church.

Feast of Our Lady of Guadalupe (December 12)

The Virgin Mary has many feast days. Both Catholic and Orthodox Christians have set aside special days in her honor. I focus here on a specifically Catholic holiday.

Catholics believe that Mary appears on Earth from time to time with instructions for the faithful. Such appearances are known as "apparitions," and every apparition has its accompanying feast day. Our Lady of Guadalupe is the most important Marian apparition in all of North and South America. This is the story associated with Our Lady of Guadalupe.

Cuauhtlatoa ("Eagle that Speaks") was a man of no pretension. He was born an Aztec Indian in 1474. He became a potter and a Christian. His Spanish name was Juan Diego. Throughout his life, he was poor.

After his wife died, Diego lived with his uncle, Juan Bernardino, in Tulpetlac. He was in his late forties when Tenochtitlán (modern-day Mexico City) was captured by the Spanish, and he was in his late fifties at the time of the following events.

Just before dawn on Saturday, December 9, 1531, Diego was on his way to church, after which he intended to run some errands. On top of a hill called Tepeyac, he met a woman of "superhuman grandeur; her garments were shining like the sun; the cliff where she rested her feet . . . resembling an anklet of precious stones, and the earth sparkled like the rainbow." [31]

The lady introduced herself as "Holy Mary, Mother of the True God." She sent Diego to the bishop of Mexico. He was supposed to tell the bishop that she wanted a temple built at Tepeyac. Diego obeyed. The bishop studied the aging Aztec. Behind the bishop's polite rejoinders, Diego sensed disbelief.

As Diego returned home, the lady met him in the exact same spot as she had in the morning. He told her that he had failed to impress the bishop and asked her to send someone else instead of him, someone of importance. She declined, and commanded him to return to the bishop the very next day with the same request.

The next day was Sunday. After Mass, Diego again called upon the bishop. The bishop asked many questions, and then requested a sign to prove Diego's claims.

When Diego left, the bishop ordered several servants to follow him. When he arrived at Tepeyac, Diego disappeared from sight. He was speaking to the lady, who told him to return the next day, when she would send with him proof for the bishop.

However, Diego's uncle was at the point of death. The doctors said they could do no more for him, and Bernardino himself requested a priest. So, on December 12, at dawn, Diego set out to fetch a priest for Bernardino. He tried to avoid the lady by taking a different route, but she appeared before him anyway.

Promising that Bernardino would be cured, the lady sent Diego to the top of Tepeyac. There, he found exquisite roses blooming even though it was winter and even though the craggy hilltop supported only thistles and weeds in the best of seasons.

Diego picked the roses and placed them in his *tilma*, or cloak. He went to present them to the bishop as a sign.

When Diego opened his tilma for the bishop, it became evident that the image of the lady had been impressed on his rough cloak. The bishop was convinced by the sign, and ordered the construction of the Tepeyac Shrine. Meanwhile, the lady appeared to Bernardino and cured him.

Today, the image on Diego's tilma is displayed in the Tepeyac Shrine. Millions of pilgrims visit Tepeyac annually, and December 12, the feast day of Our Lady of Guadalupe, is one of Mexico's most important holidays.

The Feast of the Holy Fathers (May 27)

The Holy Fathers (called the Church Fathers in the West) lived in the first Christian centuries. In Orthodox Christianity, they are the main authority for a proper understanding of the Bible and Christianity.

Who were the Holy Fathers? They include Irenaeus, Athanasius, John Chrysostom, Basil the Great, John Climacus, John of Damascus, hermits known as "the Desert Fathers," and others too numerous to name. Some were bishops in the early Church; others were monks. Some were educated in the best schools of their day, while others were illiterate. Some were martyrs. A few were women.

A Holy Father is someone who taught the faith, explained the Scriptures, and was known for holiness and virtue. A Holy Father was also believed to have received what he taught through an unbroken line of instruction going all the way back to the Apostles and the first followers of Jesus.

A Holy Father is a spiritual father. Many of the Holy Fathers had no physical descendants. Parallel to Paul's claim to have "begotten" the Corinthians in Christ (1 Corinthians 4:15), the Holy Fathers assured the "spiritual birth" of generations of Christians by teaching the true faith. Writing in the second century, Irenaeus declared, "When any person has been taught from the mouth of another, he is termed the son of him who instructs him, and the latter is called his father."[32]

It was the Holy Fathers who defined the main emphases of Eastern Christianity. In Orthodox Christianity, the Incarnation is regarded as the central event in history. Through the Incarnation, humanity is totally transformed and regenerated; through it, death is destroyed and the whole of creation is made new.

Among Orthodox Christians, salvation is not primarily "justification" (a Protestant emphasis), but rather becoming "partakers of the divine nature" (2 Peter 1:4). This concept of salvation is expressed in the famous saying, "God became man that man may become God",[33] and is called "deification" (*theosis*).

The Holy Fathers were shapers not only of doctrine, but also of a holy way of life. They taught prayer, conquest of the passions, recognition of one's sinfulness, humility, charity, visiting the sick, caring for prisoners, voluntary poverty, celibacy, participation in the liturgy, and obedience.

The Desert Fathers are especially noteworthy in this regard. They were monks and hermits. They were also, for the most part, simple and illiterate people, largely of peasant origins. Their close disciples recorded their words and actions.

The Desert Fathers were people who did without: They lived with not much sleep, few baths, only small amounts of food, little company, ragged clothes, hard work, no leisure, and absolutely no sexual contact. In silence, they heard the word of God, and in solitude, they learned the love of other people and of all creation. They were in the desert to make a pilgrimage of the heart toward Christ.

The Desert Fathers were rebels. They broke the rules of the world, which say that property and material goods are essential for life, that one who takes a vow of obedience is not free, that no one can be fully human without sex and domesticity. They were called *anchorites*, which literally means "one who withdraws from the world and does not fulfill his duties to society."

Yet they gave the world something of great value: a Christian wisdom spoken in a clear and unassuming voice. Here are two examples of their wisdom:

> (1) They said of abba[34] Macarius that he became as . . . a god upon earth, because just as God protects the world, so abba Macarius would cover the faults that he saw as though he did not see them, and those which he heard as though he did not hear them.[35]

(2) When abba Macarius was praying in his cave in the desert, a hyena suddenly appeared and began to lick his feet and taking him gently by the hem of his tunic, she drew him towards her own cave. He followed her, saying, "I wonder what this animal wants me to do?" When she had led him to her cave, she went in and brought her cubs which had been born blind. He prayed over them and returned them to the hyena with their sight healed. She in turn, by way of thankoffering, brought the man the huge skin of a ram and laid it at his feet. He smiled at her as if at a kind person and taking the skin spread it under him.[36]

9

Defining
Moments in
Christian History

Therefore the pope, when he uses the words
"plenary remission of all penalties,"
does not actually mean "all penalties,"
but only those imposed by himself....
Thus those indulgence preachers are in error
who say that a man is absolved from every
penalty and saved by papal indulgence.

—Martin Luther, Ninety-five Theses, 1517

This chapter discusses six time periods that are living memories for substantial numbers of Christians. With two exceptions, the focus is on periods that show the roots of current conflicts between Christians. The exceptions are first, Byzantium, which is discussed because it is the foundational period for Orthodoxy but little known by Western Christians, and, second, the Crusades, which are included because of their continuing appeal to the popular imagination. In chronological order, the defining moments or events covered in this chapter are 1) the early martyrs, 2) Byzantium, 3) the papacy, 4) the Crusades, 5) the Protestant Reformation, and 6) the founding visions of America.

THE EARLY MARTYRS

Many Christians think of the first Christian centuries as an age of persecution and martyrdom, a time when great heroes of the faith were willing to shed their blood so that Christianity might continue to exist and grow. There is much truth to this common perception. Although the persecutions were intermittent and many of them were local, large numbers of ordinary people, along with bishops and other church leaders, endured cruel torture and death rather than act or speak against their Christian beliefs. Christians were beheaded, burned at the stake, scourged, beaten, and mauled to death by wild animals.

Like many of the other time periods we will examine in this chapter, the memories of the persecution of the early Church are politically charged. Different Christians see the martyrs differently, and draw different lessons from this period in Christian history. Recently, any number of preachers and Websites have argued that Christians were persecuted because, being monotheists, they would acknowledge only one God, while the policy of the Roman Empire was religious pluralism.[37] This first group is opposed to current policies of religious tolerance and pluralism, and wants to use the memory of the martyrs to bolster their opposition. Their message is that Christians were persecuted because they were viewed as being religiously intolerant. On this reading of history, Christian monotheism, which excluded all other gods, necessarily led to the conclusion that Christianity should be the only religion in the empire.

One could interpret the age of the martyrs in a very different way. One might point out that the persecutions stopped when an emperor issued an edict of toleration.[38] In other words, it can be argued that the historical evidence suggests that the persecutions were the result of Roman *in*tolerance (not tolerance), and that the establishment of a policy of tolerance toward Christians halted the persecutions. From this second perspective, although Christianity ultimately became the religion of the empire, the goal of the martyrs was not religious supremacy, but simply religious freedom. Religious freedom logically entails the acceptance of religious pluralism. From this second perspective, the age of the martyrs is a plea for religious tolerance, and therefore, religious pluralism.

Can the historian determine which of these politically charged perspectives is closer to the truth? We will look at what is known of the history of the persecutions, and then return to this question.

The First Century

Historians admit that the evidence needed to reconstruct the first centuries of Christianity is fragmentary. This is not surprising. Christianity began as a small religion, one of many entering the Roman Empire from its eastern colonies. Rome allowed religions and philosophies to chart their own courses, unless their practice clashed with being a good citizen of the empire. Initially, Rome paid very little attention to the Christians.

This is not to say that Christianity had an easy time in the Roman Empire. Christians appear to have been a regular target of slander, suspicion, and verbal abuse. For the most part, it was the populace that was responsible for this, not the authorities. Christianity was in competition with both Judaism and paganism. It was the object of negative attacks from both quarters, and it returned these attacks to the extent that its own strength and numbers allowed. Rome's role in these encounters was simply to try to keep the peace.

In addition to these interreligious struggles, there were periods of governmental persecution. Until around A.D. 250, these persecutions appear to have been sporadic and local. The first on record occurred in A.D. 64, when Nero was emperor. Nero blamed the Christians for a great fire in Rome, which took place on July 19. He was apparently deflecting an accusation that he himself had ordered the blaze to clear space for his proposed Golden Palace. Tacitus's *Annals*, dating from perhaps a half century after the event, provides our earliest description of the incident.

According to Tacitus, some Christians were wrapped in the hides of wild beasts and then torn to pieces by dogs. Others were fastened to crosses and set on fire to illuminate a circus. Nero apparently believed that sentiment against the Christians would be galvanized by his actions, making him more popular. Instead, the crowd pitied the Christians and turned against Nero.

If the Book of Revelation describes first-century events (rather than the end of the world), a passage describing "Babylon" as "drunk with the blood of the saints and the blood of the witnesses to Jesus" (Revelation 17:6) actually refers to Rome's persecution of Christians. Most scholars think this passage refers to post-Neronian persecutions, but we cannot be sure of their date or location.

Second Century and Early Third Century

In the second century and the first part of the third century, we know of only occasional periods of persecution against Christians. Ignatius of Antioch wrote a letter while on his way to Rome to be executed as a Christian, and this letter was preserved. Polycarp, reputedly a disciple of the Apostle John, was martyred during the reign of Antonius (138–161). He was eighty-six years old at the time of his execution, and may well have been the last of the generation that knew and had been taught directly by the eyewitnesses of Jesus's life and resurrection. The persecutions that resulted in these deaths took place without the encouragement of the government or its officers. They were instigated by the local populace.

Christians were vulnerable to being blamed for whatever went wrong because they were regarded with suspicion by large segments of the population. Perhaps the most visible oddity of

Christians was their refusal to perform the normal demonstrations of allegiance to the empire. It was a duty of Roman subjects to participate in the public festivals and sacrifices in honor of the gods of the nation. To refuse to do so was to show a lack of concern for the welfare of the empire. (If the gods were offended by lack of worship, they might not protect Rome.) Christians, being monotheists, often absented themselves from this patriotic duty. They were called "atheists" because they refused to worship the gods. Their crime, however, was as much political as it was religious. This lack of patriotism was underlined by the fact that many Christian leaders taught that it was wrong for a Christian to serve in the army.

Because Christians were under suspicion, they gathered for worship covertly. Consequently, they were regarded as antisocial and secretive. Rumors began to circulate about their rites. Since Christians talked about eating the body and blood of Jesus, people thought they were cannibals. Because believers greeted each other with a kiss, they were thought to be either promiscuous or, perhaps, since they spoke of being members of one family, incestuous. With rumors like these circulating, it is not surprising that Christians were thought to be "notoriously depraved."[39] This alleged immorality added to the mistrust they faced because of their refusal to participate in patriotic demonstrations.

At least some Christians did engage in socially deviant behavior. Some treated their slaves as equals in Christ. They permitted women to remain single, contrary to the patriarchal expectations of Roman society. (According to Roman law, a woman had to marry and bear three children before she could be considered to have discharged her duties to the state.) An even bigger threat to society arose from the fact that some Christians believed that Paul had actually discouraged marriage, considering the single, celibate life to be a superior way of serving Jesus. The position of the father within the family was undermined by another subset of Christians. These refused to acknowledge any man as father, believing that their only true father was God (see Matthew 23:9). Others thought that a Christian could not be a teacher (see Matthew 23:8, 10).

In sum, the underlying reasons for the general mistrust of Christians that occasionally erupted into the localized persecutions of the second and early third century were (1) conflict between Christianity and Roman patriotism, (2) misinformation about Christian rites, and (3) socially deviant behavior and beliefs. Of these, the first was the most important.

Later, Empire-wide Persecutions

Beginning around the year 250, there was a change in the nature of the persecutions. The persecutions after that date were empire-wide. They were initiated and commanded by emperors, rather than started by suspicious neighbors. Once again, the reason behind the persecutions was an apparent lack of patriotism on the part of the Christians.

Decius became emperor in 249. By then, Rome had entered its period of decline. The authority of Roman rulers was in jeopardy. The army lacked discipline. Taxes increased, prices skyrocketed, and many people went bankrupt. The government paid its debts to its citizens in currency that it would not accept in payment of taxes.

In an attempt to restore order and prosperity, Decius ordered Romans to perform rituals to the gods. He hoped to rekindle the favor of the gods toward Rome. Decius didn't want martyrs; he wanted Christians to support the state by supporting the religion of the state. Anyone suspected of being a Christian was ordered to prove his or her loyalty by making sacrifices to the Roman gods in the presence of official witnesses. Christians who did so received a paper document certifying that they had sacrificed. Thousands of Christians performed the required ritual. A few who were wealthy bribed officials and received the document without actually sacrificing. Some went into hiding. The government arrested and executed some prominent Christians, including the bishops of Rome, Jerusalem, and Antioch. A later persecution under Valerian, which took place in 257 and 258, followed the same format. When it became clear that the persecutions had failed to effect any positive change in Rome's fortunes, they were discontinued.

The final persecution took place during the reign of Diocletian, in the first years of the fourth century. Christians were not allowed to assemble for worship. Bibles were burned. Churches were destroyed. Once again, Christians were ordered to sacrifice to the gods or face execution. We do not know how many Christians died in this persecution, or in any of the others. Historians recorded only a few names, generally those of prominent persons.

The empire-wide persecutions that took place between 250 and 313 were motivated by a fear that the gods were punishing Rome because Rome had failed to punish the Christians for flaunting the gods.

Conclusion

Were the persecutions the result of Christian intolerance of other religions and Christianity's rejection of religious pluralism? Or were they the result of the empire's intolerance of the Christian faith? This way of asking the question imports contemporary concerns into our study of history, and distorts our view of the early martyrs.

Christians disagreed with other religions and philosophies, but they were not intolerant of them. They were not opposed to allowing opponents to publicize their views. This is tolerance. Tolerance does not imply agreement.

On the other hand, the Roman Empire was not opposed to Christianity because it was religiously peculiar, which is to say that Rome was not acting out of religious intolerance. Rome's primary concern was the political loyalty of Christians.

Rome was religiously tolerant, but it did not have separation of church and state. Because church and state were not separate, refraining from religious activities designed to promote the welfare of the empire was tantamount to treason—it was a betrayal of one's country.

Legacies of Rome

Many ideas and institutions that are less than perfect in actuality live on in an idealized form to inspire future generations.

So it was with the Roman Empire. Even while Christians remembered the persecutions, they were impressed by Rome's size, organization, and system of law. As the empire declined, two attempts were made to declare Christianity the heir of the best that the Roman Empire had offered.

The first of these was an actual extension of the Roman Empire. It began when Emperor Constantine moved his capital to Constantinople in 333. The second resulted from the political vacuum in the West that opened when the emperor no longer resided in Rome. The bishop of Rome, later known as the pope, filled that vacuum and eventually became the highest religious and political authority in the West.

The Roman Empire in the East, reconstituted by Constantine, was known as Byzantium. It was the cradle of Orthodox Christianity. In the West, Rome became the center of Catholic Christianity.

BYZANTIUM

While Byzantium is a foundational memory for Orthodox Christians, few Western Christians know much about it. Constantine was its first emperor. Twenty-one years before Constantine moved to Constantinople, while he was in the midst of a battle fought as part of a power struggle for the throne, he saw a vision of a cross bearing the inscription, "Conquer by this." God later appeared to him in a dream and told him to make a likeness of the cross and to carry it into battle with him. Constantine won the ensuing battle at the Milvian Bridge near Rome, and took possession of the capital. During Constantine's reign, Christians were granted religious freedom in the Roman Empire.

Constantine's biographer, Eusebius, claimed that Constantine, like the Apostle Paul, had been called directly by God to embrace Christianity. The political result of this was that Constantine was believed to rule by divine right. Constantine considered himself to have been appointed by God. His government was a *theocracy* (literally, "rule of God").

The people believed that God ruled Byzantium, using the emperor as his mediator. Byzantium's emperors never claimed to be divine, but they saw themselves as God's representatives on Earth. Just as God brought the heavens into a state of peace and harmony, so the emperor was to bring all the people of the world into a state of peace and harmony. In short, God ruled in heaven and the emperor ruled on Earth.

Constantine's mother, Helena, made a pilgrimage to Jerusalem in 326. There, she supposedly discovered the cross on which Jesus had died, and the sign affixed to the cross that identified Jesus as the king of the Jews. Constantine's possession of the very cross on which Jesus had died added tremendous weight to his claim that his authority was divinely ordained.

However, Constantine only ruled in Christ's name. The real ruler of the empire was said to be Christ. Byzantium's coins bore a picture of Jesus and the inscription "Jesus Christ, King of Rulers." The ceremonies of war were considered holy, and the cross was carried into battle. Laws were passed in the name of "the Lord Jesus Christ, Our Master."

Constantinople considered itself the new Rome. Like the old Rome, it claimed to be the civilizer of the world. The practice of calling those beyond the boundaries of its civilizing influence "barbarians" began in the old Rome and continued in the new. The new Rome, however, had a further task: not just to civilize but to save. Constantine saw himself as an apostle sent by Christ to bring the Gospel to the world. He was called "the Equal of the Apostles," and this title was carved on his tomb.

The vision of an Orthodox Christian theocratic state survived even the collapse of Byzantium. By the fifteenth century, the once-Christian lands of the Middle East had all fallen under Muslim rule. Constantinople fell to the Turks in 1453, but its role was transferred to Moscow. An Orthodox Christian theocratic state existed in Russia until July 1918, when Nicholas II, the last tsar, was executed.

The patriarch of Constantinople was the head of the Orthodox Church in Byzantium. Because the East always had a strong emperor on the throne, the patriarch seldom exercised direct political power. The Church supported the political agenda of the emperor. In return, the Church was supported by state-collected taxes, and protected by the military power of the empire.

The emperor, on the other hand, had both political *and* spiritual power. He bore the title "vicar of God on Earth." The first ecumenical council was called neither by the pope nor by the patriarch of Constantinople. It was called by Emperor Constantine. The emperor presided over ecumenical councils and promulgated their decisions.

This arrangement offered establishment and protection to the Church. However, the theocratic structure of the state bestowed so much power upon the emperor that he sometimes interfered with the spiritual authority of the Church. Although technically they held only the right of nomination, emperors often virtually appointed the patriarch of Constantinople. Without the emperor's consent, no patriarch could hold office. When the Orthodox theocratic state moved to Russia in the fifteenth century, the tsars took full control of the Church. In the eighteenth century, Tsar Peter the Great abolished the patriarchate and substituted his own church structure for it.

The lack of separation of church and state resulted in the subordination of church to state. This is not uncommon. History demonstrates that churches are most forceful politically when they are not established. Established churches tend to leave religious matters in the hands of the government. This has often proven beneficial to the government, but seldom has it been helpful to religion. In this case, the Orthodox Church developed a nonactivist, otherworldly stance, which was directly related to its tendency to leave matters affecting this world in the hands of the government.

Ethics were not noticeably improved by the theocratic arrangement. Constantinople was a wealthy commercial city and its inhabitants had a reputation for sophistication and duplicity. The marriage of political power and assumed righteousness led to much cruelty. Sometimes, an ascetic or a patriarch would admonish an emperor not to harm or destroy life, but with little effect upon the behavior of rulers and their appointed officials.

Christian influence was more noticeable in culture. Byzantine art and architecture were impressive.[40] Byzantine literature was robustly religious. Libraries were filled with theology, hymns, lives of the saints, and sermons. Even though those with power seldom seemed to heed their messages, the writings of the period emphasized the importance of living a Christ-like life of gentleness and humility, pardoning the sinner, not repaying evil with evil, and forgiving one's enemies.

The monks, who were the keepers of this Christian culture, took its admonitions seriously. They were often the only ones with the courage to question the emperor. They repeatedly refused to conform to the orders of the state. This was especially noticeable during the iconoclastic period, when monks spear-headed the opposition to the government's efforts to remove the religious images from churches.

An occasional prelate took the Gospel message seriously as well. One such person was John the Almsgiver, patriarch of Alexandria in Egypt during the early years of the seventh century. John came from an eminent family in Cyprus. He was a devout layman whose wife and children died. Emperor Heraclius appointed him to be patriarch. John lived a simple and austere life, donating the revenues of his see to the poor and refugees. He humbled himself to seek reconciliation with an estranged subordinate. He never took any gift that might compromise his integrity. He attempted to enforce uniformity in weights and measures because variable standards allowed for commercial dishonesty. He increased the salaries of his stewards to render them less susceptible to bribes.

We have seen that the theocratic state in Byzantium led to a church that was politically weak even though it showed cultural strength. Things were different in the West, where the lack of a strong political system led to chaos. There, the bishop of Rome finally assumed a position of leadership, and imposed order.

THE PAPACY

The papacy is an institutional structure in which the bishop of Rome, who is usually called the pope, is the human head of the

Church. (Christ is held to be the spiritual head.) Roman Catholics subscribe to this church structure. Protestants do not. Orthodox Christians accept the pope's authority over the Western Church, but not over Orthodox believers.

The emergence and growth of the papacy is another aspect of Christian history that Christians view differently. Catholic Christians remember with pride the contributions of the papacy to European political order, civilization, and morality. Non-Catholic Christians often associate the papacy with moral and spiritual corruption. They remember the selling of indulgences to help support papal military and cultural projects, the sale of church offices, and the sometimes flagrant abuses of the priestly vow of celibacy.

As we have seen, Constantine and his successors were believed to rule by divine right. The source of this claim was Constantine's vision before the Battle of Milvian Bridge in 312. The bishops of Rome also believed that they ruled by divine appointment. The source for their claim was the Bible itself, which recorded the giving of the keys of the Kingdom, and the power to bind and loose, to Peter (Matthew 16:17–19). Peter was associated with the Church in Rome, and its bishops saw themselves as his successors.

In the East, the emperor's power was so great that it sometimes encroached upon the spiritual authority of the patriarch of Constantinople. In the West, political collapse, economic instability, and barbarian invasions followed in the wake of Constantine's abandonment of Rome as his imperial center. Only the bishop of Rome had the authority and the resources needed to impose some degree of order in this chaotic situation. He found it necessary to extend his political authority just to ensure the survival of the Church in the West. By the fourth century, the bishop of Rome was calling himself the pope (*papa*, meaning "father" or "head") of the Western Church.

The early Christian Church had developed a system of authority that rested in five patriarchs, located in Rome, Constantinople, Alexandria, Antioch, and Jerusalem. Of these five patriarchates, only Rome was in the West. For this reason, Orthodox Christians have always accepted the claim that the bishop of Rome is the head of the Western Church. However, the pope wanted to be recognized as the highest authority in the entire Christian Church, East as well as West. This, the Orthodox would not grant, for the patriarch of Constantinople was the supreme spiritual authority of Eastern Christianity. Popes began to press their claims for sovereign authority over the universal Christian Church in the fourth century.

The popes never attained authority over the entire Christian Church. After many centuries of trying to establish their authority in the West, they did manage to consolidate their power there. An important watershed occurred in the year 800, when the pope crowned the Frankish King Charlemagne as emperor. Today, as we debate the proper roles of women and foreigners in society, it is interesting to note that in 800, the Empress Irene reigned in Constantinople as "the Vicar of God on Earth," and the title of Holy Roman emperor was conferred upon a "barbarian" king. The emperor in the West assumed many of the spiritual roles of the emperor in the East: He protected and subsidized the Church, and also interfered in its life from time to time.

In the East, the patriarch did not name the emperor; if anything, the reverse was true. In the West, the pope had just named and crowned an emperor. This gave the papacy a political importance that the patriarchs had never known. However, when the Carolingian Empire (named after Charlemagne's family name) collapsed around 900, much of this political importance evaporated. There ensued a period of political intrigue and corruption. Reform movements were launched by both the emperor (who wanted to reform the papacy) and the pope (who wanted to reform the empire). This tussle evolved into a series of controversies that would last through the sixteenth century. Sometimes the pope controlled the secular ruler, and sometimes the secular ruler controlled the pope. Rather than follow the oscillating fortunes of the papacy, we will describe it at the moment of its greatest political influence.

Innocent III is generally considered the most powerful pope of all time. He was born not far from Rome in 1160 or 1161, and occupied the papacy from 1198 to 1216. Chosen to be pope at a time when the Holy Roman Empire was declining and the kingdoms of Europe were growing but not yet backed by a strong sense of nationalism, he was able to extend the powers of the papacy beyond those exercised by any of his predecessors.

Innocent III was one of the best educated men of his day. He had studied at Paris, the leading university for the study of philosophy and theology, and at Bologna, noted for its excellence in law. This man of iron will was a prodigious worker who drove himself mercilessly. He truly believed that the Christian ideal could be realized on Earth under papal guidance. He believed that Christ had appointed the pope to govern the whole world as Christ's vicar.

In 1204, the Crusaders captured Constantinople. This enabled Innocent to bring many Eastern churches under the control of Rome. Never had so much of Christianity been under the administrative control of the pope.

Innocent III asserted that the pope alone could transfer a bishop, create new dioceses, or change the boundaries of existing dioceses. He insisted upon high morals for bishops and priests. He ordered that the tithes given to support the Church should have preference over all other taxes. He insisted upon Rome's right to review important legal cases.

POPE OVERPOWERS KINGS

Pope Innocent III crowned kings and even the Holy Roman emperor. He also had the power to excommunicate any of these high-ranking officials. He forced Philip Augustus, king of France, to take back the wife he had divorced, and he compelled a Spanish king to separate from his wife because canon law prohibited the marriage. He insisted that he alone, and not the king of England, had the right to appoint the archbishop of Canterbury. In response, an angry King John seized church property and drove many English bishops into exile. Innocent excommunicated John, deposed him, and gave his crown to Philip Augustus of France. To get back his throne, John agreed to submit to papal control. He gave his kingdom to the pope, and was given it back as a papal vassal.

Under his instigation and direction, the Fourth Lateran Council (1215), the most important assembly of the Church in the Middle Ages, enacted the most comprehensive body of legislation produced by a council until the time of the Council of Trent (1545–1563). It laid down rules to improve the education of the clergy, more precisely defined several Christian doctrines, sought to raise the level of marriage and family life, condemned the taking of interest, and made it a Christian duty to confess one's sins to a priest at least once a year.

After the reign of Innocent III, the papacy entered a period of slow decline. It would never again exercise the political power it had during his reign.

Today, the pope is the earthly head of the Roman Catholic Church, over which he exercises leadership in morals and beliefs. Like certain other prominent religious leaders (such as the Dalai Lama, the spiritual leader of Tibetan Buddhism), he exercises some moral influence worldwide, but only by means of persuasion. He has no political power beyond Vatican City. He has no military and is no longer able to summon Crusaders.

THE CRUSADES

Western Christians have long cherished the memory of the Crusades. These events captured the popular imagination in their own time, and have continued to do so up to the present. Not only were the Crusades themselves immortalized as a golden age of the Christian spirit and its advance against nonbelievers, but the word *crusade* itself passed into common usage for any noble religious or moral undertaking. Thus, we had the evangelical "crusades" in the late nineteenth and early twentieth centuries, and even a recent reference to the 2003 war on Iraq as a "crusade." The actual history of the Crusades offers little to warrant this long history of positive regard. These "holy wars" were beset by serious practical and moral flaws.

Pope Urban II (1088–1099) wanted the Holy Land (the Christian holy places in Palestine) to be under Christian rule. It had been in Muslim hands since the seventh century. The pope's opportunity appeared when the Turks advanced across Asia Minor. The Turks overran Jerusalem, and stories spread about the profaning of relics and the mistreatment of Christian pilgrims. In 1095, Pope Urban II responded by organizing what was to become known as the First Crusade.

Urban II promised cancellation of debts, freedom from taxes, and eternal life to everyone who participated in the Crusade. He said Christ would lead any army engaged in battle for the Holy Land. Going on the Crusade was seen as a religious duty. In preparation for the Crusade, the pope ordered all warfare between Christian states in Europe to cease, and threatened to excommunicate (expel from the Church) anyone who did not obey. He was certainly not the first or last ruler to seize the opportunity to bring peace at home by making war somewhere else.

THE CHILDREN'S CRUSADE

The preaching against Muslims and Christian heretics fired the imaginations and triggered the emotions of children. In 1212, tens of thousands of children headed toward Jerusalem, determined to capture the Holy Land. They believed that children could work miracles that adults could not.

The Crusade had two branches, one of which originated in France and the other in Germany. The German children left the Rhine Valley in early July, and crossed the Alps, arriving at the port city of Genoa in late August. Thousands had died along the way. At Genoa, the miracle they expected failed to occur. God did not allow them to walk across the water. Disappointed and confused, the children dispersed in several directions, but few returned home. It is reported that some reached the port of Brindisi, where a Norwegian named Friso sold the boys into slavery and the girls into prostitution.

The French children walked to Marseille, where two sea captains offered to transport them to the Holy Land without charge. The children boarded seven vessels provided by the captains. A priest who accompanied them returned to Europe eighteen years later. According to his report, two of the vessels were wrecked near Sardinia in a storm. The remaining vessels turned south toward Africa and landed at the slave market at Bujelah, where the children were sold as slaves.

Note: The sources describing the Children's Crusade were written decades after the event, and show some signs of imaginative embellishment. Few question that the Crusade took place, but the details are disputed. My synopsis follows the current standard reconstruction of the event.

Urban II quickly lost control of the organization of the First Crusade. As enthusiasm for the idea spread across Europe, peasant mobs sold their land to pay for their journey, and began to march toward Jerusalem. When they ran out of food, they pillaged the local areas on their route. These Crusaders passed through Constantinople, but they were not received as conquering heroes. Fearful of being looted, Constantinople's officials rushed them out of town. The poorly prepared peasant army was left vulnerable to Turkish attacks, and most of the troops died before reaching the Holy Land.

The death of the peasants was tragic because they were Europe's farmers. Their labor was producing the growth in food and population that would make European expansion possible in the centuries ahead. Despite their usefulness to society, the peasants received little respect from the nobility. Instead, the nobles admired the knights in shining armor. Unlike the peasants, who were always useful to society, knights were only productive when there was a war. During times of peace, knights and their war games (tournaments) were a major expenditure that reaped no profit.[41]

To the Church's credit, it did what it could to discourage warfare in Europe and denounced the taking of booty as a sin. The law prohibiting the taking of booty went back to the "ban," a biblical injunction forbidding the taking of prisoners of war or spoils of war.[42] It guarded against self-interested warfare by making sure that no one profited from going to war. When the knights substituted tournaments for the warfare that the Church had condemned, the Church denounced these as well. The knights ignored the Church's complaints about the tournaments, which had become a favorite pastime of the nobility. Now, however, the knights needed a way to demonstrate their usefulness to society and to show that they were good for more than mere entertainment. The Crusades were the answer. From five thousand to ten thousand knights and between twenty-five thousand and fifty thousand other soldiers volunteered for the First Crusade.

Although the Muslim overlords of the Holy Land were the

target of the First Crusade, Jews frequently became the victims instead. Jews were ordered to make contributions to the Crusade. Sometimes they were forced to be baptized. As the Crusaders passed through various towns in Europe, Jews were often attacked and murdered.

Not all Christians were so callous. At Speyer, a city along the Rhine River, a Catholic bishop protected the Jews by cutting off the hands of anyone who killed a Jew. Jews sometimes took refuge in a bishop's palace, but at Worms, Germany, Crusaders broke into the bishop's palace and killed the approximately five hundred Jews hidden there. Other massacres of Jews occurred at Mainz and Cologne.

The battle cry of the Crusaders was "*Deus le volt!*" ("God wills it!"). The knights and soldiers were better fighters than the peasants. They managed to conquer the Holy Land in 1099. They took gold, silver, horses, and mules as spoils of war. They invaded houses in search of loot. They murdered anyone who did not flee Jerusalem. Enflamed by the mistaken belief that the Jews (not the Romans) had killed Christ, they massacred Jews. Many Jews took refuge in Jerusalem's main synagogue, only to be burned to death. Some Crusaders had the decency to be shamed by the brutality.

The Second Crusade (1147–1149) was called after Muslims captured the city of Edessa in what is now southern Turkey. It failed to return the city to Christendom. In 1187, the great Muslim leader Saladin recaptured Jerusalem. The Third Crusade (1189–1191), led by King Richard the Lionhearted of England, failed to win back Jerusalem. After Saladin died in 1193, Pope Innocent III decided to seize the moment; he called for a new crusade to take back Jerusalem from the Muslims.

Like the First Crusade, the Fourth Crusade soon slipped out of papal control. Venetian merchants, vying with Constantinople for trade with the Muslims, offered transportation to the Crusaders in exchange for their capture of the port town of Zara and its deliverance to the Venetians. Learning of this arrangement, Constantinople rebelled against the Crusaders'

"KILL THEM ALL—GOD KNOWS HIS OWN!"

After the Fourth Crusade, Pope Innocent III turned his attention away from the Holy Land and toward problems closer to Rome. A movement whose members were known as Albigenses (from the city of Albi in southern France) or Cathari ("the pure") was spreading through northern Spain, southern France, and northern Italy.

The Cathari believed that there are two eternal powers, a good power and a bad power. The bad power created the visible world and the good power created the spiritual world. They also believed that there were two churches. Their own church was the true Church of Jesus Christ, and it was good. They considered the Church of Rome the evil church. The Cathari believed that the flesh is evil. Therefore, Christ could not have had a real body. Consequently, he could not really have died on the cross.

Those who had fully embraced the Cathari way of life were called "perfect." The perfect never had sexual relations. They never ate meat, milk, or eggs. They were forbidden to engage in war or to own property. They were zealous missionaries.

In 1179, the Third Lateran Council declared a crusade against the Cathari. It was the first crusade carried out against people who called themselves Christians. In 1181, a crusading army moved against the Cathari with some success. It was soon disbanded, however, and the Cathari once again flourished. When a papal legate was murdered in Cathari lands in 1208, however, Innocent III took advantage of the widespread reaction of horror to call up another crusading army.

Heresy was a capital offense, and some of the Crusaders took upon themselves the role of executioner. At Beziers, when the Crusaders asked their leader how they could distinguish Christians who were loyal to Rome from the Cathari, he reportedly responded, "Kill them all— God knows his own!" The Crusaders appear to have followed orders, for twenty thousand men, women, and children were massacred at Beziers.

Like most persecutions, this one failed to eliminate its target group. The Cathari remained in existence for almost two more centuries, despite persistent efforts by the Church to destroy them.

presence. The Crusaders retaliated by unleashing a three-day orgy of rape and plunder. Orthodox Christian convents and churches were looted. Fire destroyed much of the city. The Crusaders set up their own king in Constantinople. In accordance with an agreement made beforehand, half the booty taken in Constantinople went to the Venetians.

Pope Innocent III was overjoyed to hear the news of the fall of Constantinople to the Crusaders, for that brought a significant part of Eastern Christendom under the control of the Roman Church. When he learned of the atrocities committed by the Crusaders, he was shocked—but not shocked enough to consider relinquishing the city.

Roman rule would only last until 1261. In the meantime, much of the territory formerly controlled by Constantinople was lost to its opportunistic neighbors. As a whole, Christendom was weakened, not strengthened, by the Fourth Crusade.

THE PROTESTANT REFORMATION

The sixteenth-century Reformation was the foundational period for Protestant Christianity. The two greatest reformers of that time were Martin Luther, who initiated the Reformation, and John Calvin, the father of the Presbyterian and Reformed churches.

Martin Luther

Martin Luther (1483–1546) was of German peasant heritage. He was a man of strong convictions and decisive actions.

Luther's father wanted him to become a lawyer. Luther began law school, but left in the midst of his studies to enter an Augustinian monastery. He strictly observed all the rules and penances of the order, but still wasn't sure that he had achieved salvation. Luther had a great fear of the wrath of God, and felt no assurance of God's mercy and grace. These feelings had not dissipated by the time he became a professor at the university in Wittenberg, Germany, but he did take some spiritual comfort in the preparation of his lectures on the Bible.

Luther's inner anxiety was finally put to rest by a sentence from Paul's Letter to the Romans: "The just shall live by faith" (Romans 1:17). It led Luther to understand profoundly that God cannot be cajoled into being merciful through good works. God is a wise father, not one who is easily manipulated. Nothing we can do, nothing we can give him, will fool God into thinking that we are not sinners. Luther retained a place for good works, but he thought they should come after, not before, our knowledge that we are saved if we believe in God. Any gift given to God should come from a heart filled with gratitude, not fear. Like any father, God doesn't want his children to try to buy his love. He wants them to know and rejoice in his love. Like any father, God loves us even though we are imperfect.

Luther ignited the fires of reform without really intending to do so. When a papal agent by the name of Johann Tetzel arrived in Wittenberg selling indulgences, Luther attacked the practice in a piece of writing that he posted on the door of the castle church. (An indulgence is the forgiveness of the punishment for sin in exchange for prayers or good work. It is *not* the forgiveness of sin itself.) The Ninety-five Theses, as Luther's document is called, appeared on October 31, 1517.

In the Ninety-five Theses, Luther was inviting academic debate on his positions. This was a common practice at the time. He never anticipated the degree or kinds of interest he received. Luther caught the attention not only of academics, but of the general populace as well. The university press was unable to keep up with the demand for copies of his Theses that poured in from every part of Germany. Clearly, there was a widespread desire for reform, which had been awaiting only the right person to mobilize it. Luther was that person.

Luther was ordered to appear before the pope for trial and discipline. A German prince, Frederick of Saxony, decided to protect and defend his countryman, however. He succeeded in having the requirement modified so that Luther would only have to appear before a papal legate at Augsburg.

As Luther prepared for his defense before the papal legate, his thinking continued to develop. Soon, he no longer questioned the sale of indulgences alone, but also the entire view of penance and good works as a kind of "transaction" that could get a person out of debt to God.[43] He also questioned the need for a priest to act as a mediator between a Christian and God in the matter of repentance. Luther believed that true repentance is answered with an inward assurance of God's forgiveness. Forgiveness comes through a direct personal relationship with Christ, and through Christ with God, not by confessing one's sins to a priest.

As Luther continued to criticize the existing religious authorities, he was obviously left with the question of where religious authority should be invested. His answer was: in the Bible alone. The Catholic Church continues to believe that the meaning of the Bible is not self-evident, and that the Holy Spirit guides the Church to a correct understanding of Scripture. Luther, on the other hand, believed that the meaning of the Scriptures was clear, and that the Holy Spirit guided the individual believer in his or her understanding. This further removed the necessity of the Church as a mediator between God and humanity.

When Luther appeared before the papal legate, he was ordered to recant (to renounce his position and submit to the teaching authority of the Church). He refused, and escaped back to Wittenberg. Rome was busy with other issues, and forgot about Luther for a while. However, when Luther found himself forced to admit in the middle of a debate that he thought the Church had erred when it executed John Hus (an earlier reformer) in 1415, the pope issued a bull of condemnation against him.

In 1521, Luther was summoned to appear before the Diet of Worms to defend his position. In bold words that have rung down through history, Luther, with his life in the balance, addressed the emperor and the delegates of the Church. He said that he refused to retract his position unless he could be convinced by Scripture alone that he was in error. He would not accept reasoning based on papal pronouncements or Church councils.

Because he had appeared at Worms under a guarantee of safe conduct, Luther was allowed to leave unharmed. It was understood, however, that he was subject to arrest as soon as he arrived home. The Diet ordered Luther to surrender and forbade anyone else to shelter him. It also banned the reading of his writings. Fortunately for Luther, Frederick of Saxony had sent envoys to seize him on his way home. He was taken to Wartburg Castle, where he had to remain hidden for fear of his life. Luther used his confinement to translate the New Testament into German so that the common people would be able to read it.

The Edict of Worms was never enforced, and Luther, with Germany largely supporting him, emerged from hiding. Some princes, emboldened by this turn of events, renounced their allegiance to the pope and joined Luther's cause.

By the time Luther died in 1546, his reforms had spread across most of Germany (with some exceptions in the south), and into Scandinavia and the Baltic States. Today, the Lutheran Church is one of the world's largest Christian denominations, with approximately 64 million members.

John Calvin

John Calvin (1509–1564) was responsible for creating the ethos that once dominated European Protestantism, and which continues to dominate American religious culture. Calvin is remembered for his precise intellect, and even more for his vision of a moral society based on biblical principles.

Calvin was French by birth, and a lawyer and humanist by education. By the time he was twenty-six years old, Calvin had published a Reformation classic, *The Institutes of the Christian Religion*. Its crystal-clear statement of the beliefs of the reformers moved Calvin into a position of leadership in the Protestant movement. The *Institutes* were revised and supplemented throughout the course of Calvin's life. They were destined to serve as the foundation of Presbyterianism.

Calvin's later public policies flowed from the religious

convictions defined in the *Institutes*. These convictions included the following:

> *First*, the sovereignty and the glory of God. God is almighty, all-knowing, and all-holy. He wills whatever happens in the natural world and in human history. Since human beings are not capable of fully understanding God's will, his decisions may appear to us to be arbitrary. But in actuality God is holy and righteous, and all of his decisions are just.

> *Second*, since human understanding is dimmed by original sin, we must rely heavily on Scripture for knowledge, and especially for knowledge of God.

> *Third*, original sin corrupts every part of human nature. Bodies are doomed to die, minds to darkness, and wills to sinful desires. Since that is the case, human beings are incapable of doing anything to work their way out of their sinful state.

> *Fourth*, but this does not mean that all is lost. God has fore-ordained some, but not all, to salvation. God decides the eternal destiny of human beings even before they are born. This is known as the doctrine of predestination.

> *Fifth*, those who are saved are saved through faith in Christ Jesus.[44]

In 1536, William Farel persuaded Calvin to participate in the building of the new Reformed Church in Geneva, Switzerland. Calvin developed the social organization of the Church and the city. He was the first major political thinker to model social organization entirely on biblical principles.

At first, the Genevans were unwilling to accept the reform measures, and in 1538, the opposition succeeded in banishing Calvin and Farel from the city. Calvin moved to Strasbourg, France, where he wrote commentaries on the Bible.

By 1541, Geneva had decided to accept Calvin's leadership, and the city asked him to return. Calvin set about the task of establishing a theocracy[45] in Geneva. The Bible, believed to be the sole source of God's law, was adopted as the law of the city. Human beings were to interpret and apply God's law, thereby preserving the orderly world that God had ordained.

Calvin believed strongly in duty and self-discipline. He believed that one should live in the awareness that one is always in God's eye. He thought people lowered themselves beneath their God-given dignity if they engaged in excessive drinking, card playing, dancing, or partying. Yet Calvin was not an ascetic. He wanted only as much self-denial as was necessary for self-discipline. He wrote that only an "inhuman philosophy" would limit the use of God's gifts to necessity.[46] John Knox, the founder of Presbyterianism, was reportedly somewhat shocked to find Calvin bowling on a Sunday.

Calvin bequeathed to Geneva a trained ministry and a people well enough educated to be able to give a clear account of their faith. Geneva became the most important Protestant center of Europe in the sixteenth century. Protestants who were driven out of France, England, Scotland, and the Netherlands took refuge in Calvin's city. Scholars moved there by free choice. The city increased in population from thirteen thousand to nineteen thousand residents.

Most of the refugees who arrived in Geneva came with general Protestant convictions and left as thoroughly committed Calvinists. They became, in effect, Calvinist missionaries. It is probably for this reason that Calvinism became the dominant branch of Protestantism from the seventeenth century onward.

The Church of Scotland is thoroughly Calvinistic in theology and practice, having been modeled on the church in Geneva. The Puritans of England were Calvinists, and so were the Puritans of New England.

Today, Calvin's most direct descendants in the United States are the Reformed and Presbyterian churches. His indirect influence on American culture is far greater. It can be seen in the American emphases on organization and discipline, in America's "work ethic" and its frugality, and in the desire on the part of many Americans to embody biblical principles in

American educational systems, in American culture, and in U.S. political leadership.

Postlude

The sixteenth-century Reformation is indeed a glorious memory in Christian history. It brought much-needed reforms to the original Church. It is sad, however, that it has left a legacy of division among Christians. The divide between Catholics and Protestants was so deep that, for centuries, each denied that the other knew God's salvation. How deep, in reality, are the differences between Protestants and Catholics?

First, we should note that both types of Christianity have needed reform over time. There were many reform movements in the Catholic Church, both before and since the Protestant Reformation. Protestants, too, have needed to make alterations within their churches. The Puritans were attempting to reform Protestant Christianity, as were the nineteenth-century evangelical reformers in the United States.

Second, it would be inaccurate to think that Catholics would disagree with all or even most of the teachings of Martin Luther and John Calvin. Luther found a theological soul mate in Augustine, who is also a significant figure in the Catholic Church. Catholics would agree with much of Luther's theology, and much of Calvin's as well.

Differences do remain, of course. Catholics emphasize free will while Calvinists emphasize God's control over all things. Lutherans say that the Bible is the sole source of ultimate authority, whereas Catholics believe that one needs an additional authority to determine which interpretation of the Bible is correct. These differences, however, are no greater than the differences between Lutherans and Calvinists. Lutherans believe in the real presence of Christ in the Eucharist, while Calvinists do not. Calvinists believe it is both possible and appropriate to organize a Christian state around biblical law, whereas Lutherans are opposed to the mingling of religion and secular law.

And so it goes. Christians will always have their disagreements.

But they also share a tremendous amount of common ground, and this is no less true of Protestants and Catholics than it is of differing Catholic points of view or differing Protestant points of view.

CHRISTIAN VISIONS OF AMERICA

Some Americans want the United States to be a religiously plural nation, while others believe it should be a Christian nation. These two visions of America began as early as the colonial period. In this section, we will examine the origins of both of these ideas of America.

The Puritan Vision

One of the earliest visions of what America could or should be was that of Massachusetts Bay Colony. Governor John Winthrop and the other colonists of Massachusetts Bay were Puritans. They believed the society they were about to establish in the New World should be based on the Bible. They described themselves as "the new Israel," seeing themselves as a Christian people who would live according to the law of God. The idea that America is or should be "a Christian nation," "a biblical nation," or "a covenanted people" began in Massachusetts Bay.

Although Puritanism died out, Puritan ideals continued to inform American culture. Even in the twentieth century, presidential inaugural addresses sometimes referred to the United States as a "city on a hill," a phrase taken from John Winthrop's speech on board the *Arbella* (the ship that brought the Puritans to America) in 1630. Because the Puritan vision in general, and this one speech in particular, have played such a large role in American Christian self-understanding, we will examine Winthrop's speech here.[47]

Winthrop's address begins with a rather harsh-sounding statement about God's providence. God, he says, has willed some people to be rich and others poor, some to have power and dignity, and others to remain in submission to the powerful. This is not an excuse for brutal domination or callous indifference, however.

Rather, it is the opening scene in a vast panorama of Christian love. God has so ordered the world, Winthrop says, because he wants the rich to serve the poor by dispensing God's gifts to them.

The work of the Holy Spirit is manifest in this world of differences, restraining the greed of the rich and mighty, and the resentment and anger of the poor and powerless; building the virtues of mercy and gentleness in the powerful and wealthy, and the virtues of faith, patience, and obedience in the meek and poor. God has planned things so that "every man might have need of others, and from hence they might be all knit more nearly together in the bonds of brotherly affection."

It is plain, Winthrop continues, "that no man is made more honorable than another or more wealthy, etc., out of any particular and singular respect to himself, but for the glory of his Creator and the common good of the creature, Man." God, as master, continues to own what he distributes to his servants for their use. The servant of God serves God by freely giving to others what he or she has received from God. The servant *owes* this service to God; it is not a matter of the servant's generosity.

Human beings are supposed to live according to both the Law of Nature (the moral law) and the Law of Grace (the Gospel). The Law of Nature commands people to love their neighbors as themselves, for this is the basis of the moral law that regulates all our dealings with other human beings. The law requires helping another person (Christian or not) in any need or distress. This Law of Nature is based on the fact that all human beings share the same flesh (they are all descendants of Adam and Eve), and they are all made in the image of God (Genesis 1:27).

One is expected to do good to all, but especially to the household of faith. One is not to tempt God by leaving another Christian dependent upon help "by miraculous or extraordinary means."

The rule of mercy demands giving, lending, and forgiving a debt. In ordinary times, one may give out of one's abundance. In extraordinary times, however, a person must give from what he or she needs for personal sustenance—one cannot give too much. Against the objection that one must save for his or her children, Winthrop answers that giving to the poor is a loan to God, and the Lord will repay the giver and his or her family a hundredfold. Another objector states the need to have something set aside for future hard times. Winthrop responds with the Gospel command not to lay up treasures upon Earth (Matthew 6:19). However, if the Church or our brother has no need of them, "it is not only lawful but necessary to lay up as Joseph did [see Genesis 41]," so that one will have something to give when it is needed and called upon by God.

The rules of lending allow one to deal with a brother who has the means to repay according to the "way of commerce" and the "rule of justice." If he has no means to repay a loan, one must simply give him what he needs and not expect repayment. One must not excuse oneself from the duty to lend to someone in need simply because that person may not be able to repay the loan. Furthermore, whether given by way of commerce or mercy, one must forgive a debt if the borrower has no means of repayment. In times of peril, it may even be necessary to sell everything and hold all things in common, with no one having anything to call his or her own.

All this is demanded by love, which is the fulfillment of God's law. Love is like a ligament. It is what knits the body together and makes it work. Original sin is the selfishness with which all people are born. When Christ claims someone as his own, he infuses a new principle—namely, love of God and neighbor. Love is the fruit of the new birth, and "none can have it but the new creature." It is by love that we are healed, and by love that we are raised from the dead.

If the new society about to be born is to succeed, public interests must "oversway" all private interests, "for it is a true rule that particular estates cannot subsist in the ruin of the public." Winthrop also warned his people that they would be dissembling with God if they were to embrace this present world (rather than the next world) and seek earthly wealth and fame for themselves and their children. If they did so, God would break out in wrath against them.

"The only way to avoid this shipwreck," Winthrop concluded,

> is to follow the counsel of Micah, to do justly, to love mercy,
> to walk humbly with our God. . . . For we must consider that
> we shall be as a city upon a hill. The eyes of all people are
> upon us. So that if we shall deal falsely with our God in this
> work we have undertaken, and so cause Him to withdraw
> His present help from us, we shall be made a story and a
> by-word through the world.

Long before America became the richest nation in the world,
long before there even was a country called the United States,
John Winthrop predicted that America's greatest temptation to
idolatry would lie in its worship of pleasure and profits:

> But if our hearts shall turn away, so that we will not obey, but
> shall be seduced, and worship other Gods, our pleasure and
> profits, and serve them; it is propounded unto us this day, we
> shall surely perish out of the good land whither we pass over
> this vast sea to possess it.

The Pluralist Vision

Unfortunately, not everyone who came to settle in the American
colonies was as high-minded as Governor Winthrop. It
wasn't long before the Massachusetts Bay Colony had hanged
four Quakers in an attempt to eliminate "alien" elements.
Similarly, Virginia persecuted Baptists. While what is now
New York was still called New Netherlands, Governor Peter
Stuyvesant attempted to "cleanse" his colony of Lutherans,
Quakers, and Jews.

Out of this bloody turmoil, a new Christian vision emerged.
The Mid-Atlantic colonies of New York, New Jersey, Pennsylvania,
Delaware, and Maryland began to experiment with religious
toleration, religious pluralism, the voluntary church, and separation of church and state.

After Governor Stuyvesant commanded the expulsion of
Quakers from the territory of New Netherlands in 1656, the

inhabitants of the town of Flushing replied with a biblically based refusal to comply with his orders. "Out of Christ God," wrote the Flushing residents,

> is a consuming fire, and it is a fearful thing to fall into the hands of the living God. We desire therefore . . . not to judge least we be judged, . . . but rather let every man stand and fall to his own Master. Wee are bounde by the Law to Doe good unto all men. . . . that which is of God will stand, and that which is of man will come to nothing.

The residents of Flushing specifically referred to non-Christians (Jews and Muslims) in their statement of peaceful coexistence, saying, "they are considered the sonnes of Adam" and

> love, peace and liberty . . . extending to all in Christ Jesus, condemns hatred, war and bondage . . . our desire is not to offend one of his [Christ's] little ones, in whatsoever form, name or title he appears in, . . . but [we] shall be glad to see anything of God in any of them, desiring to doe unto all men as we desire all men should doe unto us, . . . for our Savior saith this is the law and the prophets.

This statement of tolerance was written two days after Christmas in 1657.[48] Other demands for religious tolerance appeared even earlier.

The Maryland Toleration Act (1649) stipulates legal penalties for calling anyone residing or trading in its territory a "heretic," "schismatic," "idolator," "Puritan," "Independent," "popish priest," "Jesuited priest," or any name or term that might appear to be a reproach to the person's religion. The penalty for engaging in the prohibited conduct was ten shillings or a public whipping, followed by imprisonment without bail until the guilty party publicly begged forgiveness from the offended party.

Earlier still, in 1644, Roger Williams (founder of Rhode Island) argued against what he called "the doctrine of persecution for the cause of conscience." According to Williams, Jesus Christ, who is Prince of Peace, neither requires nor accepts the blood of any person on account of his or her religious faith or lack thereof. "The doctrine of persecution for cause of conscience is proved guilty of all the blood of the souls crying for vengeance under the altar" (a reference to Revelation 6:9–10). God, claims Williams, never intended to create another kingdom or civil state in the world that would be a second Israel. Rather, the coming of Christ heralded a new direction in history. Since then, according to Williams, God grants freedom of conscience and worship to all (he specifically mentions pagans, Jews, Turks, and those opposed to Christianity). Untruth is, indeed, to be battled, but only with the one sword that avails in the realm of the spirit—namely, the sword of the word of God. Williams also argues for a clear separation of the powers of the Church versus those of the state.[49]

CONCLUSION

We conclude this chapter where we began, with the problem of Christian exclusivity versus religious pluralism. A large part of American identity is tied up with being a Christian nation, which entails at least some degree of exclusion. However, the United States is equally committed to religious tolerance and freedom of religion, which logically entails religious pluralism. This contemporary American dilemma has its roots in the differing Christian visions of the Puritans and the pluralists during the colonial period. Both visions were based on the Bible.

The question lingers: What *is* America's God-given mission? Is it to Christianize the world? Or is it to build a nation where people can be free to worship God (or not worship) as they choose?

10

Christianity in the World Today

And Jesus came up and spoke to them, saying,
"All authority has been given to Me in heaven and on
earth. Go therefore and make disciples of all the nations,
baptizing them in the name of the Father and
the Son and the Holy Spirit, teaching them
to observe all that I commanded you; and lo,
I am with you always, even to the end of the age."

—Matthew 28:18–20

RELIGION RETURNS

In the High Middle Ages (approximately 1000–1200), the Christian Church was the supreme political as well as religious authority in Europe. During the Reformation and modern periods, however, political authority was increasingly vested in the nation-state. In the twentieth century, Christianity's role in public life was further diminished by secularism in the West and by communism in China, Central Asia, Southeast Asia, Russia, and Eastern Europe.

Under Communist regimes, religions were barely allowed to function. Even in those nation-states that protected religious freedom, religion usually played less of a role in the political, intellectual, and social spheres of life than it had prior to the modern period. By the middle of the twentieth century, religion was substantially relegated to the private and cultural spheres of life. This was especially evident in the United States and Western Europe.

A number of signs indicate that this trend is now reversing. The grip of antireligious political philosophies weakened considerably during the last decade of the twentieth century. The collapse of the former Soviet Union was especially significant in this regard. The emergence of a resurgent Islam on the political scene, and its criticism of the secular West, focused media attention on the political and social power of religion in a bloc of nations that, by world standards, possesses a considerable amount of affluence and influence. The strength of religiously conservative political activism in the United States in recent decades surprised many, but it was not an aberration—both religious conservatism and religious activism are increasing worldwide.

Spearheaded by the Dalai Lama's universally recognized spiritual presence, a politically active form of Buddhism emerged in the second half of the twentieth century. It operated not only among Tibetan Buddhists, but also in Southeast Asia and in the West. Confucianism has been acclaimed as a significant contributor to Asian economic success. Indigenous traditions have fought for, and sometimes received, the return of their traditional lands. A mere half century after people wondered whether Christianity would survive in a increasingly secularized world, no one any longer questions the continuance of Christianity. On the other hand, people do wonder aloud about the future of the nation-state.

A RELIGIOUS SENSE OF IDENTITY

A recent flurry of speculation suggests that governments in coming decades will have less and less control over the flow of information, technology, diseases, migrants, weapons, and financial transactions across their borders. Political analysts also surmise that the very concept of "belonging" to a particular state will probably erode.

This speculation looms most ominously in newly independent countries, especially those challenged by internal divisions. The boundaries of such countries were often drawn for the benefit of a colonial power. They do not reflect the social and cultural identities of the peoples who live within the lines on the map.

Any one of the world religions might provide a ready repository for a sense of identity adrift in a weak nation-state. The world religions in general, and Christianity in particular, can offer a sense of identity with impressive spatial and temporal extension. Other than large corporations, a religion is the only international body to which most people can aspire to belong. Christianity has the additional advantage of being traditionally, not newly, international. The first institution of any kind to operate on a global scale may well have been the Roman Catholic Church (beginning around 1600, with the expansion into the Western Hemisphere and Asia).

A world religion like Christianity also offers temporal extension

The twenty-first century will almost certainly be regarded by future historians as a century in which religion replaced ideology as the prime animating and destructive force in human affairs, guiding attitudes to political liberty and obligation, concepts of nationhood, and, of course, conflicts and wars.

—Philip Jenkins, Distinguished Professor of History and Religious Studies, Pennsylvania State University for one's sense of identity. Although nation-states and kingdoms can usually survive at most a few centuries before being replaced by new states or dynasties, the major religions of the world have endured for millennia. The laws and codes of conduct of the religions have proved more durable than those of nations. Somewhere in the back of their minds, people realize this.

It is not surprising, then, that when admittedly human institutions like the nation-states falter, people look toward those institutions that they believe were established by God. Once again, as in the pre-modern era, increasing numbers of people find comfort in the vision of a supranational order in which their political, social, and personal identities would be substantially defined by religious loyalties.

PROVIDING SECURITY AND SUPPORT IN A CHAOTIC WORLD

In addition to a sense of identity, Christianity often provides a sense of social security and economic support. New Christian churches in the "Two-Thirds World" (Africa, Asia, and Latin America) gain members only to the degree that the church is able to drive out the demons of oppression and poverty. The fact that these new churches and their members belong to an international organization that redistributes wealth (in the form of charitable giving) is a critical factor.

The role of Christianity as a security net is likely to increase if the gap between people's needs and governments' ability to fill them widens. According to historian Peter Brown, Christianity succeeded in the Roman Empire only when it outdistanced the empire in protecting and providing support for its subjects. If one's own tribe is not the group favored by the government of an ethnically or religiously divided nation-state, or if one's nation is expending resources in the interests of political stability rather than on welfare, one may well have to look elsewhere for support. Today, as once in the Roman Empire, it often happens that being a member of an active Christian church brings more tangible benefits than being a citizen of a country.

A return to the faiths will not necessarily bring comfort and security to the world, however. In the midst of poverty, epidemics, unemployment, and homelessness, tensions can run high. These frustrations may channel themselves into religious terrorism. In a weak nation-state, there is little control over this type of religious response to negative political, social, and economic situations.

On the other hand, any unscrupulous government could easily attempt to deflect the anger of its unemployed youth by convincing them to fight in the cause of God against an external enemy. This would shift critical scrutiny away from the government, at least temporarily. National or ethnic loyalties, when stoked by religious passion, have led many to march to their death singing the praises of God and country. This is an especially dangerous possibility in light of the spread of weapons of mass destruction.

Whether the increasing significance of religion brings hope or terror to the world will depend on how well their incredible energies can be channeled. The world faiths are staging an international comeback. Will they return to the public sphere bearing peace or war, competition or cooperation, charity or chastisement?

THE NEW CHRISTIAN DEMOGRAPHICS

Christianity leads the world religions in terms of both numbers and geographic distribution. That there will be more Christians than members of any other faith in the twenty-first century, and that they will be found everywhere on the face of the planet, seems certain. By 2025, the number of Christians in the world is expected to reach 2.6 billion, making Christianity by far the world's largest faith. This mega-faith will not be simply a larger sea of the same old faces.

In 1900, 80 percent of the world's Christians lived in Europe or North America. In 2000, 60 percent lived in Asia, Africa, or Latin America (480 million in Latin America, 360 million in Africa, 313 million in Asia, and only 260 million in North America). In 1900,

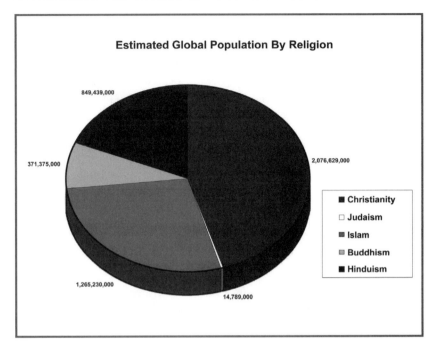

Estimated Global Population By Religion

849,439,000

371,375,000

2,076,629,000

■ Christianity
□ Judaism
▦ Islam
▨ Buddhism
■ Hinduism

1,265,230,000

14,789,000

This pie chart shows the estimated global population of adherents in each of the five largest religions—Christianity, Judaism, Islam, Buddhism, and Hinduism. With more than 2 billion believers, Christianity is by far the world's most common and widespread faith.

most Christians lived in developed nations. Today, the majority lives in developing nations.

By 2025, 50 percent of all Christians will live in Africa and Latin America, and another 17 percent will be in Asia. Europeans and Euro-Americans are already in the minority in the Roman Catholic Church. Current projections place close to three-quarters of all Catholics in Africa, Asia, and Latin America by 2025.

By around 2050, the United States will still have more Christians than any other single nation. But the southward swing of populations is evident from the roll call of what are projected to be the other leading Christian nations: Mexico, Brazil, Nigeria, the Democratic Republic of the Congo, Ethiopia, and the Philippines.

African Christianity

Christianity is growing fastest in sub-Saharan Africa. The first European missionaries ventured south of the Sahara in the fifteenth century, but Africa was not dependent on them for long. The spread of Christianity in Africa over the last five centuries was accomplished primarily by African Christians, not by European or American missionaries.

Contemporary African Christianity can be divided into three main groups: Roman Catholic churches, Protestant churches, and African Indigenous churches (AICs). Roman Catholic churches were founded by Catholic missionary orders. For the most part, they have remained within the worldwide Catholic Church and have not branched out on their own as independent churches. In the last half of the twentieth century, they assumed parity with Catholic delegations from other continents. Indeed, there has been considerable speculation that Pope John Paul II's successor will be from Africa.

Protestant churches were founded by European and American Protestant missionaries. They stress the authority of the Bible and the need for an individual relationship with Jesus as one's personal savior. They encompass within their broad range both Anglican churches, which have much in common with Roman Catholic churches, and Pentecostal churches, which are virtually indistinguishable from AICs.

AICs are variously called African Indigenous churches, African Independent churches, or African Initiated churches. They typically derive from a Protestant mission context, but at some point, they struck out on an independent path and now function without reference to overseas churches. Though many of them follow the practices of traditional Protestant denominations, others combine elements of Christianity with tribal religions.

The Kimbanguist Church

The Kimbanguist Church of Zaire is an example of an AIC. Its founder, Simon Kimbangu, was a member of the English Baptist Mission Church. He believed he had received a call to initiate a preaching and healing mission in the lower Congo. His followers were drawn from both Protestant churches and indigenous African religions.

Kimbangu believed in healing by the laying on of hands. He taught strict observance of Mosaic Law, and repudiated sorcery, magic, charms, and witches. He prohibited polygyny. His success in attracting followers caused alarm among both church and state authorities.

In June 1921, the government judged the movement out of control, banned it, and exiled members to remote rural areas. They arrested Kimbangu, only to have the prophet escape in a mysterious manner. His followers called it a miracle. In September, Kimbangu surrendered voluntarily to the authorities. He was sentenced to death for hostility against the state. His sentence was later commuted to life in prison. Kimbangu died in prison in 1950.

After Kimbangu's death, his church continued to spread. Ultimately, the state despaired of stamping it out, and decided to legalize it instead. The Kimbanguist Church is now one of three Christian groups recognized by the state, the other

THE LORD'S RESISTANCE ARMY

The Lord's Resistance Army (LRA) is a Christian fundamentalist group. It claims as its mission the creation of a theocratic state based on the Ten Commandments. It operates in Uganda and Sudan. From bases in southern Sudan, its armed guerrillas pour into Uganda to loot and attack. In just six months in 1997, the LRA was responsible for four hundred deaths in northern Uganda, and the displacement of two hundred thousand farmers.

The LRA specializes in abducting children, who are trained and used as fighters for the LRA's cause. Amnesty International estimates that five thousand children have been kidnapped and escaped from the LRA, with approximately another five thousand still being held in southern Sudan. From the Ugandan Army's point of view, an abducted child who has been given military training, and is pointing a gun at an Ugandan, becomes a legitimate target.

two being the Roman Catholic Church and the Church of Christ in Zaire. The Kimbanguist Church became a member of the World Council of Churches (WCC) in 1969. It was the first "new religion" to be seated on that international body. (A "new religion" is a religion that began within the last two centuries.)

GROWING CONSERVATISM

The worldwide Christianity of the twenty-first century will be a new Christian mix, with different proportions of the traditional denominations, and with new, often syncretistic, types of Christianity. (*Syncretism* means putting together beliefs and practices from different religions.) In general, Protestant Christianity in the Southern Hemisphere is more conservative than Euro-American Protestantism. The highest growth rates in Southern Protestantism are found among evangelicals and Pentecostals, groups that fall on the conservative end of the American religious spectrum.

The growth of Pentecostalism has been truly phenomenal. Emerging as an independent Christian movement only about a century ago, it now lays claim to around 500 million members, most of them in the Southern Hemisphere. Projections suggest that there may be as many as a billion Pentecostals by 2040, at which point this one branch of Christianity alone would outnumber the world's Buddhists and roughly equal the number of Hindus.

Although the Vatican accuses their bishops and theologians of being too liberal, the Catholics who make up the Latin American and Asian masses practice a faith that resembles pre–Vatican II Catholicism. It is hierarchical, respecting the authority of bishops and priests. It is also orthodox in faith and morals, and inclined toward traditional Catholic devotions.

Jehovah's Witnesses (The Watchtower Tract and Bible Society) and Mormons (The Church of Jesus Christ of Latter-day Saints), both viewed as only marginally Christian in the United States, are showing strong growth rates worldwide. They are socially conservative in their orientation, and will add to the growing conservatism of global Christianity.

SYNCRETISM

Despite its conservatism, the Christianity of the Two-Thirds World is often syncretistic, giving rise to a sometimes creative, sometimes chaotic, mix of religions and cultures. As early as the sixteenth century, slaves captured in western Africa and brought to Cuba combined their native Yoruba religion with Catholicism; the result was Santeria. In Santeria, *orishas* (emissaries of the one supreme god, whose name was *Olurun*) were merged with the Catholic saints. A similar mixing of native religion with Catholicism has occurred among the Mayan Indians in Guatemala and southern Mexico.

In Japan, where Christians comprise only about one percent of the population, indigenous Christian movements exist alongside the traditional denominations. Most indigenous Japanese Christian movements teach that God's self-revelation did not end with the Bible. These Japanese Christians believe that God continues to reveal ever deeper truths to those willing to be led by the ongoing work of the Holy Spirit. These more profound truths, they say, have not yet been grasped by the Western churches.

Further examples of syncretism are everywhere. Following the Confucian tradition of honoring one's ancestors, Chinese Catholics may venerate their ancestors after Mass. Christians may continue to address tribal deities. In India, sin is readily identified with bad karma, and Indian Christians frequently believe that Jesus died to save them from reincarnation. A Christian service in India may begin with the congregation chanting "Om," the sacred sound of Hinduism.

Putting the Bible in the hands of people from various cultures invites both variant interpretations and new adaptations of its message. This, in turn, brings worries about the maintenance of doctrinal orthodoxy. The pope has chided Catholic missionaries for incorporating elements of Asian spirituality. The missionaries themselves felt it was more important to focus attention on the courage demonstrated by Asian converts, who regularly face ostracism and persecution.

PERSECUTIONS
China
With the inauguration of the Cultural Revolution in 1966 under Communist leader Mao Zedong, churches in China were closed, Bibles burned, and priests and ministers sent to work camps for reeducation. All public worship was banned. However, Chinese Christians continued to worship secretly in private homes known as "house churches." When China softened its stance against religion in the 1980s, it was discovered that indigenous forms of Christianity had survived the Cultural Revolution and were still being practiced.

The Chinese government now pays at least vocal homage to the concept of religious freedom. Nonetheless, Protestant houses of worship continue to be destroyed, frequently accompanied by accusations that the Christian group was a "dangerous cult." And two-thirds of China's Catholic Christians belong to the underground church rather than the official Chinese Catholic Church, because the latter requires severing contact with Rome.

Soviet Union
The Orthodox Christians of the former Soviet Union existed in a state of siege from October 1917, when the Bolsheviks seized power, until the dissolution of the Soviet Union in 1991. Dozens of bishops, thousands of priests, monks, and nuns, and tens of thousands of laity were martyred. Immediately prior to the beginning of World War II (1939–1945), only four Russian Orthodox bishops had not been confined to prisons or concentration camps. Across the vast span of the Soviet Union, only several hundred churches remained open for worship. Although the intensity of the persecution varied from period to period, the basic attitude of the Communist authorities toward religious belief never changed: Religion was both an error and a prejudice, and it needed to be exterminated.

The rebuilding of Orthodox Christianity in Russia and Eastern Europe is now in progress. Many church buildings, confiscated decades ago and used for nonreligious purposes, have been repossessed by the faithful. They are often in a state of advanced decay.

Western evangelical Christians poured into formerly Communist territories. They were willing to donate time and labor to reconstruct the physical structures of the churches, a service for which the Orthodox were very grateful. Orthodox Christians were offended, however, by the narrow definition of Christianity possessed by many evangelicals, who seemed to think that Orthodox Christianity was not true Christianity. A full-page advertisement that appeared in the September 16, 1991, issue of *Christianity Today* was particularly offensive. Paid for by the International Bible Society, it appealed to readers "to help the people of the Soviet Union meet the real Jesus."

Japan

Francis Xavier, a Jesuit priest, established a Christian community in Japan in the sixteenth century. However, the Jesuits were driven out of Japan by a severe persecution in the next century. When missionaries returned to Japan in the mid-nineteenth century, they discovered a thriving community of "hidden Christians" at Nagasaki.

In 1889, the Meiji Constitution guaranteed religious freedom. By the 1930s, however, the government labeled Shinto beliefs and practices as "patriotic" in an attempt to unify the country. Shinto became a symbol of nationality, and those who did not embrace it were considered ideologically deviant. Christianity was declared a "dangerous" belief system, primarily because of its idea of the coming Kingdom of God. It was feared that this belief might lead to political revolution.

The postwar constitution of Japan (1947) separated church and state and provided for religious freedom. It came too late,

The [Communist] Party cannot be neutral towards religion. It conducts an anti-religious struggle against all and any religious prejudices.

—Joseph Stalin, leader of the Soviet Union, 1924–1953

however, for the oldest center of Christianity in Japan. The Christian community that had survived two centuries in hiding was obliterated by the atomic bomb dropped on Nagasaki by the United States in August 1945, at the end of World War II.

Contemporary Martyrs

In May 2000, Anglican, Lutheran, Russian Orthodox, and Pentecostal Christians joined Pope John Paul II in an ecumenical event that paid tribute to the Christian martyrs of the twentieth century. The Vatican has drawn up a list of more than twelve thousand twentieth-century Christian martyrs, but the names on it have not been made public. The pope stated that most of the martyrs on the list were "unknown soldiers."

In a separate ceremony in 1998, ten twentieth-century Christian martyrs were commemorated with statues at Westminster Abbey in London. Those honored were:

- Grand Duchess Elizabeth of Russia, killed by the Bolsheviks in 1918

- Manche Masemola, an Anglican catechumen from South Africa killed by her parents in 1928 (she was sixteen years old when she died)

- Maximillian Kolbe, a Roman Catholic priest killed by the Nazis in 1941

A MODERN-DAY MARTYR

Father A.T. Thomas was a Jesuit priest in the Indian state of Bihar. He helped nearly two hundred Dalit ("untouchable") families win back rights to land that had been snatched by the upper social classes. He even convinced a local court to send a group of land-grabbers to jail. In October 1997, he was abducted while attempting to protect a peasant from armed intruders. His headless body was discovered several days later, limbs broken and covered with burn marks. The Keralite priest was forty-six years old.

- Lucian Tapiede, an Anglican from Papua New Guinea, killed during the Japanese invasion in 1941

- Dietrich Bonhoeffer, a Lutheran pastor and theologian killed by the Nazis in 1945

- Esther John, a Presbyterian evangelist from Pakistan, killed by a Muslim extremist in 1960

- Martin Luther King, Jr., a Baptist minister and leader of the civil rights movement in the United States, assassinated in 1968

- Wang Zhiming, a pastor and evangelist killed during the Chinese Cultural Revolution in 1973

- Janani Luwum, an Anglican archbishop assassinated in Uganda in 1977 during the rule of Idi Amin

- Oscar Romero, a Roman Catholic archbishop in El Salvador, assassinated in 1980

CHRISTIANITY'S FUTURE

Christianity has passed through the refiner's fires of secularism and persecution. In many areas of the world, twentieth-century Christians saw more obscurity than fame, more oppression than opportunity. As the twenty-first century dawns, however, Christianity appears poised to exercise a leadership role in world affairs.

Christianity will remain the largest of the world's religions for the foreseeable future. It is currently characterized by a balance of conservatism and cultural adaptability. Like all resurgent religious traditions, it needs to take care to avoid fanaticism and extremism. If it can successfully avoid these dangers, it has much to contribute as a broad-based international influence in a global environment.

27 B.C.	End of Roman Republic and beginning of Roman Empire
c. 6 B.C.	Jesus of Nazareth born
c. A.D. 27–33	Jesus of Nazareth crucified
c. A.D. 50–100	Books of the New Testament written
60	Christian churches established in most of the major cities of the Roman Empire
70	Destruction of the Jerusalem Temple
64–313	Era of the early Christian martyrs
284	Diocletian's reign as emperor of Rome begins; this becomes year one on the Coptic Christian calendar

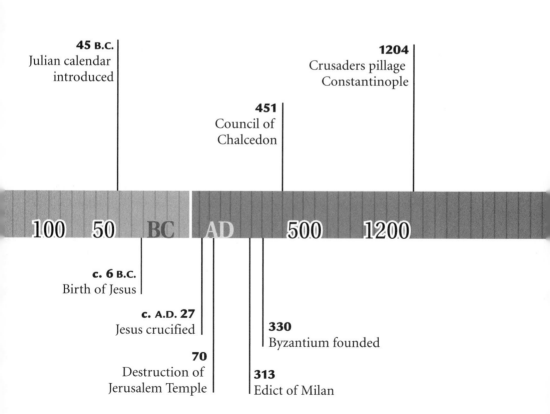

45 B.C.
Julian calendar
introduced

1204
Crusaders pillage
Constantinople

451
Council of
Chalcedon

100   50   BC   AD   500   1200

c. 6 B.C.
Birth of Jesus

c. A.D. 27
Jesus crucified

330
Byzantium founded

70
Destruction of
Jerusalem Temple

313
Edict of Milan

c. 300 Armenia becomes the first nation to officially declare itself a Christian nation

313 Edict of Milan ends persecution of Christians in the Roman Empire

330 Constantinople founded by Constantine I; Byzantium (the Byzantine or Eastern Roman Empire) founded when Constantine moves his capital to Constantinople

350 December 25 is established as the date for Christmas by Julius I, bishop of Rome

c. 400 Bible translated into Latin by St. Jerome (c. 331–420)

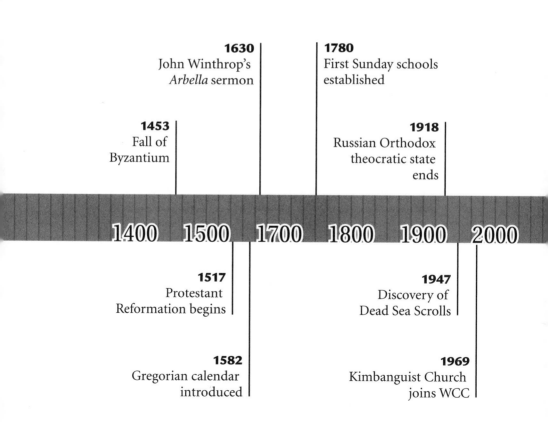

1630
John Winthrop's
Arbella sermon

1780
First Sunday schools
established

1453
Fall of
Byzantium

1918
Russian Orthodox
theocratic state
ends

1400 **1500** **1700** **1800** **1900** **2000**

1517
Protestant
Reformation begins

1947
Discovery of
Dead Sea Scrolls

1582
Gregorian calendar
introduced

1969
Kimbanguist Church
joins WCC

CHRONOLOGY

451	Council of Chalcedon defines the combination of divine and human natures in Jesus
532–537	Construction of Hagia Sophia
726–842	Age of iconoclasm ("breaking of images")
787	Seventh Ecumenical Council endorses veneration of icons
1095	First Crusade called for by Pope Urban II
1096–1099	First Crusade
1147–1149	Second Crusade
1179–1208	Crusades against the Cathari
1182–1226	Life of Francis of Assisi
1189–1191	Third Crusade
1198–1215	Papacy of Innocent III, most powerful of the medieval popes
Thirteenth century	Gothic cathedrals built
1202–1204	Fourth Crusade
1204	Crusaders capture and pillage Constantinople
1212	Children's Crusade
1410	The Lord Chief Justice of England asserts that education is the Church's business, and does not come under the jurisdiction of common law
1453	On May 29, Byzantium falls when Ottoman Turks capture Constantinople
1480	Ivan III, grand duke of Moscow, establishes the Russian Orthodox theocratic state, successor to Byzantium
1483–1546	Life of Martin Luther
1509–1564	Life of John Calvin

CHRONOLOGY

1517 On October 31, the Protestant Reformation begins when Martin Luther posts his Ninety-five Theses in Wittenberg

1531 On December 9, first apparition of Our Lady of Guadalupe to Juan Diego

1534 England renounces the authority of the pope with the Act of Supremacy

1541 John Calvin establishes a theocracy in Geneva

1582 Pope Gregory XIII introduces Gregorian calendar

1611 King James Version of the Bible is issued

1630 A sermon by John Winthrop articulates the Puritan vision of America

1639 First Baptist community in the United States founded at Providence, Rhode Island, by Roger Williams

1649 Maryland Toleration Act lays out punishments for acts of religious intolerance

1657 Flushing Remonstrance provides biblical arguments for religious tolerance

1703–1791 Life of John Wesley, founder of Methodism

1707–1788 Life of Charles Wesley, Methodist hymn writer

1750 Christianity becomes more widespread than any previous religion

1780 First official Sunday school established in Gloucester, England, by Robert Raikes

1852 Harriet Beecher Stowe's *Uncle Tom's Cabin* mobilizes antislavery sentiment

1883 On November 26, Sojourner Truth dies

CHRONOLOGY

c. 1900 Henry Thacker Burleigh arranges and popularizes African-American spirituals; Woman's Christian Temperance Union (WCTU) campaigns against consumption of alcohol; Pentecostalism begins at the Azusa Street Church in Los Angeles

1917–1991 The Orthodox churches of Russia and Eastern Europe exist under Communist oppression and persecution

1918 In July, the Orthodox Christian theocratic state in Russia ends with the execution of Nicholas II, the last tsar; on November 7, birth of Billy Graham, leading evangelical of the twentieth century

1947 Dead Sea Scrolls discovered near Qumran

1956 Billy Graham founds *Christianity Today*, a popular evangelical periodical

1969 Kimbanguist Church of Zaire is first "new religion" to become a member of the World Council of Churches (WCC)

1996 U.S. Congress decides that parents do *not* need a teaching certificate to homeschool their children

CHAPTER 1: Introduction

1 The phrase comes from Irenaeus, who is recognized as a Father of the Church by both Eastern and Western Christians.

2 There are, however, small churches that have a Catholic style of liturgy and theology, but are not in communion with Rome. There are also small, distinctive Eastern groups of Catholic Christians that are in union with Rome (e.g., the Ukrainian Catholic Church and the Chaldean Uniate Church of Iraq, which is centered in Baghdad).

3 Quotation available online at *http://www.peacemakers.net/unity/ DueProcess.htm*.

4 Author interview with the Reverend Edward Schreur, Pastor of Faith Reformed Church in Brookings, South Dakota.

5 Bob Jones criticism of Billy Graham, available online at *http://www.christianitytoday.com/ch/ 2000/001/1.12.html*.

6 Billy Graham response to Jones quoted at Ibid.

7 Author interview with the Reverend Dan Campbell.

CHAPTER 2: Jesus of Nazareth

8 Quotation available online at *http://www. pbs.org/wgbh/pages/frontline/shows/ religion/etc/script1.html*.

CHAPTER 6: Growing up Christian

9 I interviewed a number of people while preparing to write this chapter. In most cases, I will use only their first names. In a few instances, the interviewee requested that I further conceal their identity. In those cases, I have used a fictitious first name.

10 Author interview with Ruth Manson.

11 Author interview with the Reverend Edward Schreur, Pastor of Faith Reformed Church in Brookings, South Dakota.

12 Author interview with Tamera Schreur.

13 Author interview with Rachel Manzer.

14 Author interview with anonymous Lakota woman.

15 There is a Catholic equivalent, which is called "Religious Ed" (short for "religious education"). The curriculum for Religious Ed classes is chosen by each diocese. A typical curriculum would include New Testament, Hebrew Scriptures, sacraments, the liturgical calendar, saints, morality, the creed, liturgy and worship, and a semester covering church history.

16 "The African American Journey: A History of the Negro Sunday School," available online at *http://www2. worldbook.com/features/features. asp?feature=aajourney&page=html/ bh118a.html&direct=yes*.

17 D. Wadman, "The case of the excluded middle," Ph.D. thesis presented to the University of Exeter, April 1996. Quoted in "The history of Catholic schools," available online at *http://www.tasc.ac.uk/depart/EDUCATIO/ catholic/ite/pgcesec/2002/history.doc*.

18 Author interview with Sue Engelmann.

CHAPTER 7: Christian Cultural Expressions

19 From Paul the Silentiary, "Descriptio S. Sophiae," available online at the *Internet Medieval Sourcebook*, Paul Halsall (March 1996) *http://www.fordham.edu/ halsall/sbook.html*.

20 In Martin Luther's foreword to Georg Rhau's *Symphoniae iucundai*, 1538 (a collection of fifty-two hymns). Quoted in "The Musical Reforms of Martin Luther," by Charles K. Moss, M.M.Ed., M.Mus., available online at *http://classicalmus.hispeed.com/ articles/luther.html*.

21 While stringed instruments can be tuned to exact pitch, organs and pianos have to use a compromise tuning that is not as precise.

22 John Calvin, "Preface to the Psalter," available online at *http://www.fpcr.org/ blue_banner_articles/calvinps.htm*.

23 Ibid.

24 Calvin on Psalm 81:3, quoted in "The Regulative Principle of Worship in History," by Reg Barrow, available online at *http://www.swrb.com/newslett/ actualnls/CRTPWors.htm*.

25 Regarding the accusations against both Catholics and other Protestants, see Reg Barrow, "The Regulative Principle of Worship in History," available online at *http://www.swrb.com/newslett/actualnls/CRTPWors.htm.*

26 Ibid.

27 I am indebted for much of the factual information on WCTU to "The Religious Movements Homepage, The University of Virginia," and in particular to Sarah K. Roberts's article on "Woman's Christian Temperance Union (WCTU)." The Religious Movements Homepage is available online at *http://religious-movements.lib.virginia.edu/.* The WCTU article can be found online at *http://religiousmovements.lib.virginia.edu/nrms/wctu.html.*

28 "Harriet Beecher Stowe, 1811–1896." Available online at *http://americancivilwar.com/women/hbs.html.*

29 "Who was Sojourner Truth?" Available online at *http://www.noho.com/sojourner/whowas.html.*

CHAPTER 8: Calendar and Holidays

30 As an alternative to this formula, a priest may say, "Repent and believe in the good news."

31 From the *Nican Mopohua,* written in Nahuatl, the Aztec language, around 1550. The original is lost, but a copy was published in Nahuatl by Luis Lasso de la Vega in 1649. This citation is from an English translation of the 1649 copy, published on the "Our Lady of Guadalupe" Website. Available online at *http://www.sancta.org/nican.html.*

32 Ireneaus, *Against Heresies* 4.41.2. Full text of *Against Heresies* available online at *http://www.gnosis.org/library/advh1.htm.*

33 Ibid.

34 *Abba* means "father."

35 From CoptNet, "The Paradise of the Desert Fathers." Available online at *http://pharos.bu.edu/CN/articles/ParadiseOfDesertFathers.txt.*

36 Ibid.

CHAPTER 9: Defining Moments in Christian History

37 See, e.g., Rick Wade, "Persecution in the Early Church," available online at *http://www.probe.org/docs/persecution.html,* and "Roman Religion," *http://www.roman-empire.net/religion/religion.html.*

38 This was the effect of Gallienus's Edict of Toleration, and also of Constantine's Edict of Milan (313) and his later edict of toleration, which applied to the entire Roman Empire (324).

39 Tacitus, *The Annals of Imperial Rome,* XIII.32. London: Penguin, 1989, p. 365.

40 See chapter 7 for discussions of Byzantine art and architecture.

41 Many countries use militias rather than standing armies for this very reason. In the United States, the National Guard is an example of such a militia. The United States maintains the National Guard in addition to full-time military personnel.

42 See, e.g., Joshua 6:17–18 on the destruction of Jericho, and 1 Samuel 15, in which Saul disobeys the ban and consequently loses his kingship.

43 The Church had for centuries been involved in economic as well as political transactions in Europe. It could remit the financial debt that one person owed another, thereby freeing the debtor from a life of struggle trying to get out of debt. It perhaps seemed natural to the Church to extend this economic practice into the spiritual sphere. The merits of Christ and the saints were like a giant "bank" in heaven that would never run dry. Sinners, unable to work their own way out of their indebtedness to God, could be freed through the grace of these merits. The use of this economic paradigm reflects the impact of the growth of capitalism on medieval society. The emergence of capitalism was partly responsible for the growth in power of the papacy in the twelfth and thirteenth centuries, and for the building of the huge cathedrals to which Protestants would later object. It was perhaps only natural at this point in history for the Church to extend the newly emerging

economic paradigm into the spiritual sphere. Luther was right to point out the theological errors in that enterprise. Ironically, the Catholic Church, shamed by Luther's criticisms, has forever after refused to get too closely entangled with capitalism, but Protestantism and capitalism, on the other hand, have grown together.

44 John Calvin's *Institutes of the Christian Religion* is available online at *http://www.bible.org/docs/history/calvin/institut/httoc.htm.*

45 *Theocracy* literally means "the rule of God." We have seen that the Byzantine theocracy rested on the belief that the emperor was divinely appointed to rule. Calvin's theocracy was different. It claimed to be a "rule of God" because it was governed by God's law as found in the Bible.

46 Available online at *http://www.ucalgary.ca/~nurelweb/papers/irving/cal-cul.html.*

47 Winthrop's speech is titled "A Model of Christian Charity." It can be found online at *http://www.winthropsociety.org/doc_charity.php.*

48 The full text of the Flushing Remonstrance may be found online at *http://www.newsday.com/extras/lihistory/vault/hs301a1v.htm.*

49 Roger Williams's argument for the separation of church and state may be found online at *http://www.constitution.org/bcp.religlib.htm.*

BIBLIOGRAPHY

INTERVIEWS

Author's personal interviews with:

Madeleine Andrawis

Mary Andrawis

Reverend Dan Campbell

Charles W. Canaan, D.M.A., Professor of Music and Director of
Choral Activity, South Dakota State University

Sue Engelmann

Reverend Dennis Erickson

Mother Marcia Hunter

Reverend David Johnson

Reverend Teri Johnson

Reverend Dave Kaufmann

Ruth Manson

Rachel Manzer

Barb Nelson

Reverend David Schould

Reverend Edward Schreur

Tamera Schreur

Father Michael Wensing

The author also interviewed a Lakota woman, who prefers to remain
anonymous.

BOOKS

Albanese, Catherine L. *America, Religions and Religion*, 3rd ed.
Wadsworth Publishing Company, 1999.

Barr, David L. *New Testament Story: An Introduction*, 3rd ed. Wadsworth,
2002.

Breuilly, Elizabeth, Joanne O'Brien, and Martin Palmer. *Religions of the
World: The Illustrated Guide to Origins, Beliefs, Traditions, and Festivals*.
Facts on File, Inc., 1997.

Corbett, Julia Mitchell. *Religion in America*, 4th ed. Prentice Hall, 2000.

Gilbert, Olive, ed. *The Narrative of Sojourner Truth*, 1850. Available online at http://www.digital.library.upenn.edu/women.truth/1850.

Harris, Ian, Stuart Mews, Paul Morris, and John Shepherd. *Contemporary Religions: A World Guide*. The Longman Group UK Limited, 1992.

Jenkins, Philip. *The Next Christendom: The Coming of Global Christianity*. Oxford University Press, 2002.

Latourette, Kenneth S. *A History of Christianity, Volume I: Beginnings to 1500*, Rev. ed. HarperSanFrancisco, 1975.

Molloy, Michael. *Experiencing the World's Religions: Tradition, Challenge, and Change*, 2nd ed. Mayfield Publishing Company, 2000.

Noss, David S. *A History of the World's Religions*, 11th ed. Prentice Hall, 2003.

Sloyan, Gerard S. *Jesus in Focus: A Life in Its Setting*. Twenty-Third Publications, 1983.

Weaver, Mary Jo. *Introduction to Christianity*, 3rd ed. Wadsworth Publishing Company, 1998.

ARTICLES

Bahr, Ann Marie, "American culture indebted to John Calvin," *The Brookings Register* (July 5, 2001), p. A7.

———, "A mother's heart changes the world," *The Brookings Register* (June 13, 2002), p. A6.

———, "Aztec Indian receives most influential Marian vision in the Americas," *The Brookings Register* (December 12, 2002), p. A6.

———, "Christmas banned, then recreated," *The Brookings Register* (December 26, 2002), p. A7.

BIBLIOGRAPHY

———, "Christmas between church and cheer: The origin of Christianity's most popular holiday," *The Brookings Register* (December 19, 2002), p. A5.

———, "Coptic Christians celebrate new year," *The Brookings Register* (September 14, 2000), p. A7.

———, "Each culture has its own calendar," *The Brookings Register* (May 11, 2000), p. A6.

———, "Evangelical women fight alcoholism, forge new roles for women," *The Brookings Register* (November 15, 2001).

———, "Sojourner Truth: the devil's formidable foe," *The Brookings Register* (November 21, 2002), p. A6.

"The fight for God," *The Economist* (December 21, 2002), pp. 32–36.

Jenkins, Philip, "The Next Christianity," *The Atlantic Monthly* (October 2002), pp. 53–68.

Lyman, Isabel, "Homeschooling: Back to the Future?" *Cato Policy Analysis*, No. 294 (January 7, 1998). Available online at http://www.cato.org/cgi-bin/scripts/printtech.cgi/pubs/pas/pa-294.html.

Muller, Karen, "A history lesson of Sunday school," *York Daily Record* (January 4, 2003).

WEBSITES

Agnosticism/Atheism, "Religion in Zaire: The Kimbanguist Church," 2002. http://atheism.about.com/library/world/KZ/bl_ZaireKimbanguist.htm.

Barrow, Reg, "The Regulative Principle of Worship in History." http://www.swrb.com/newslett/actualnls/CRTPWors.htm.

BBC, "Martyrs of the modern era," 1998. http://news.bbc.co.uk/1/hi/uk/129587.stm.

———, "Uganda's rebels keep the faith," 2002. http://news.bbc.co.uk/1/hi/world/africa/2083241.stm.

Burris, Skylar H., "Biblical Imagery in Gerard Manley Hopkins's 'God's Grandeur.'"
http://65.107.211.206/hopkins/burris1.html.

"Calvin's Preface to the Psalter."
http://www.fpcr.org/blue_banner_articles/calvinps.htm.

Christian History Institute, "Magnificent Medieval Cathedrals: The Bible in Stone," *Glimpses* Issue #117.
http://www.gospelcom.net/chi/GLIMPSEF/Glimpses/glmps117.shtml.

Clifford, Alan C., "The Christian Bookshop: Charles Wesley (1707–88)."
http://www.christian-bookshop.co.uk/free.biogs.cwesley.htm.

CoptNet, "The Paradise of the Desert Fathers."
http://pharos.bu.edu/CN/articles/ParadiseOfDesertFathers.txt.

"Curriculum."
http://www.home-schooling-information-software.com/Home-Schooling-Information-Curriculum.html.

Dogali, Reverend Michael, "The Eucharist."
http://www.spirituality.org/issue21/pg04.html.

"Encyclopedia Coptica: The Christian Coptic Orthodox Church Of Egypt."
http://pharos.bu.edu/.

Episcopal Church of Taiwan, "What Do Anglicans Believe?"
http://www.episcopalchurch.org/taiwan/goodshepherd/belief.html.

Halsall, Paul, "Paul the Silentiary: 'Descriptio S. Sophiae,'" *Internet Medieval Sourcebook.*
http://www.fordham.edu/halsall/source/paulsilent-hagsoph1.html.

"Harriet Beecher Stowe, 1811–1896."
http://americancivilwar.com/women.hbs.html.

"The history of Catholic schools."
http://www.tasc.ac.uk/depart/EDUCATIO/catholic/ite/pgcesec/2002/history.doc.

BIBLIOGRAPHY

"Home Schooling Statistics."
http://www.home-schooling-information-software.com/Home-Schooling-Statistics.html.

"Interlupe, The Appearance."
http://pp.terra.com.mx/msalazar/1-e.html.

International Education Exchange (IEDX), "What Should I Know About Homeschooling?"
http://iedx.org/article_1.asp?ContentID'FAQ1&Section-GroupID'NEWS.

Kauflin, Bob, "Our Debt to Charles Wesley."
http://crosswalk.com/faith/ministry_articles/worshipmatters/1108746.html.

Korzilius, Lester, "Medieval Cathedrals and their meanings."
http://www.lesterkorzilius.com/pubs/ma/medieval/01.htm.

McDonald, Dale, PBVM, PhD, "Annual Report on Catholic Elementary and Secondary Schools, United States Catholic Elementary and Secondary School Statistics 2002–2002."
http://www.ncea.org/newinfo/catholicschooldata/annualreport.asp.

McKay, Jim, "Confirmation."
http://home.epix.net/~areopag/confirm.htm.

"The Mission of the Russian Orthodox Church After Communism," *East-West Church & Ministry Report.* Vol. 1 No. 3 (Summer 1993).
http://www.samford.edu/groups/global/ewcmreport/articles/ew01301.htm.

Moss, Charles K., M.M.ED., M.Mus., "The Musical Reforms of Martin Luther."
http://classicalmus.hispeed.com/articles/luther.html.

National Catholic Educational Association, "NCEA Mission Statement," 2003.
http://www.ncea.org/about/mission/.

http://www.negrospirituals.com.

"Our Lady of Guadalupe: The Apparitions and the Miracle."
http://www.sancta.org/nican.html.

Rahman, Maseeh, "Modern-Day Martyrs," *Time* (May 11, 1998),
Vol. 151, No. 18.
http://www.time.com/time/magazine/1998/int/980511/
asia.modernday_martyrs.a34.html.

"Religious Bodies of the World with at least 1 Million Adherents."
http://www.adherents.com/adh_rb.html.

Roberts, Sarah K., "Woman's Christian Temperance Union (WCTU)."
(This article is part of the Religious Movements Homepage at the
University of Virginia.)
http://religiousmovements.lib.virginia.edu/nrms/wctu.html.

"Sacraments: Communion."
http://www.catholicireland.net/communion/communion.shtml.

"Sacraments: Reconciliation."
http://www.catholicireland.net/reconciliation/reconc.shtml.

Shipley, Courtenay V., "The Effects of Martin Luther on Music," 1998.
http://www.vanderbilt.edu/Blair/Courses/MUSL242/f98/mluther.htm.

Smith, Frank E., "Europe, Church and Economic Growth to 1300."
http://www.fsmitha.com/h3/h10eu.htm.

Smith, Mark K., "Hannah More: Sunday schools, education and youth
work," *The Encyclopedia of Informal Education.*
http://www.infed.org/thinkers.more.htm.

———, "Quakers and adult schools."
http://www.infed.org/walking/wa-quak.htm.

———, "Robert Raikes and Sunday Schools."
http://www.infed.org/walking/wa-raikes.htm.

Stowe, Harriet Beecher, "Sojourner Truth, the Libyan Sibyl."
http://eserver.org/fiction/sojourner-truth.txt.

BIBLIOGRAPHY

"The Victorian Web: 'God's Grandeur' by Gerard Manley Hopkins."
http://65.107.211.206/hopkins/hopkins3.html.

Waltermulder, Dave, J. Amber Hudlin, and Ellie Kaufman, "A Tradition
of Spirituals."
http://www.gwu.edu/~e73afram/dw-ah-ek.html.

Ware of Dioklei, Bishop Kallistos, "The Orthodox Christian year,
a cycle of feasts and fasts," (Web page of the Greek Orthodox
Archdiocese of Australia).
http://home.it.com.au/~jgrapsas/pages/Year.html.

Williams, Craven E., "Origins: Singing Our Faith."
http://www.gborocollege.edu/prescorner/singing.html.

World Book, Inc., 2003, "The African American Journey: A History
of the Negro Sunday School."
http://www2.worldbook.com/features/aajourney/html/bh118a.html.

"Worship and Prayer," a Website maintained by the Orthodox
community in Great Britain and Western and Central Europe.
http://www.orthodox.clara.net/worship.htm.

Zampino, Mother Jean, "The Amazing Life and Hymns of Charles
Wesley," © Life in Jesus Community, 1998.
http://www.lifeinjesus.org/art_wesley.html.

PRIMARY SOURCES

Calvin, John. *Calvin's Commentaries*. Baker House, 1984.

———. *Institutes of the Christian Religion*, ed. Tony Lane and Hilary Osborne. Baker Book House, 1987.

Luther, Martin. *By Faith Alone*. Penguin USA, 1998.

———. *Martin Luther, Selections from His Writings*, ed. John Dillenberger. Anchor, 1958.

Soldier, Lydia Whirlwind, "Memories," *Shaping Survival: Essays by Four American Indian Tribal Women*, ed. Lanniko L. Lee, Florestine Kiyukanpi Renville, Karen Lone Hill, and Lydia Whirlwind Soldier. The Scarecrow Press, Inc., 2001.

Truth, Sojourner, as told to Olive Gilbert, *The Narrative of Sojourner Truth*, published in 1850. Available online at http://docsouth.unc.edu/neh/truth50/menu.html.

Wesley, John. *John Wesley's Sermons: An Anthology*, ed. Albert C. Outler and Richard P. Heitzenrater. Abingdon Press, 1991.

SECONDARY SOURCES

Breuilly, Elizabeth, Joanne O'Brien, and Martin Palmer. *Religions of the World: The Illustrated Guide to Origins, Beliefs, Traditions, and Festivals*. Facts on File, Inc., 1997.

Corbett, Julia Mitchel. *Religion in America*, 4th ed. Prentice Hall, 2000.

Jenkins, Philip. *The Next Christendom: The Coming of Global Christianity*. Oxford University Press, 2002.

Nystrom, Bradley P., and David P. Nystrom. *The History of Christianity: An Introduction*. McGraw-Hill, 2004.

Riches, John. *The Bible: A Very Sort Introduction*. Oxford University Press, 2000.

WEBSITES
Amiens Cathedral Project
http://www.learn.columbia.edu/Mcahweb/index-frame.html.

FURTHER READING

Anderson, Ken, "The Music of the Church"
http://www.kenanderson.net/bible/music_of_church.html.

BBC, "A state apart: An interactive chronicle of the Northern
Ireland conflict"
http://www.bbc.co.uk/northernireland/education/stateapart/
agreement/reconciliation/

Dawkins, Richard, "Children must choose their own beliefs," *The
Observer* (Sunday, December 30, 2001).
http://www.world-of-dawkins.com/Dawkings/Work/Articles/
2001-12-30morris_letter.htm.

Harriet Beecher Stowe Center, "Harriet's Life & Times"
http://www.harrietbeecherstowecenter.org/life.

"Harriet Beecher Stowe: Uncle Tom's Cabin"
http://www.uwm.edu/Dept/Library/special/exhibits/clastext/clspg149.htm.

Pogatchnik, Shawn, "Irish religious bigotry starts early, study shows,"
St. Paul Pioneer Press (Tuesday, June 25, 2002).
http://www.twincities.com./mld/pioneerpress/living/religion/
3536759.htm.

Shipley, Courtenay V., "The Effects of Martin Luther on Music," 1988.
http://www.vanderbilt.edu/Blair/Courses/MUSL242/f98/mluther.htm.

Truth, Sojourner, "Ain't I A Woman?"
http://www.nisto.com/wct/who/sojourn.html.

WebExhibits: "Calendars through the Ages"
http://webexhibits.org/calendars/calendar.html.

Willard, Frances, "We Sang Rock of Ages"
http://historymatters.gmu.edu/text/1707a-willard.html.

"Woman's Christian Temperance Union"
http://www.wctu.org/earlyhistory.html.

INDEX

Bible
  and Catholics, 7, 8
  and evangelicals, 14
  Hebrew (Old Testament), 22,
    23, 35
  and Lutherans, 10, 157
  and Protestants, 7, 8, 9, 71
  and Puritans, 158-161
Bible camp, 74
bishop of Rome, 139, 142.
    See also papacy
bishops, 5, 7, 8, 12, 73
Board schools, 83-84
Bob Jones University, 14
Bonhoeffer, Dietrich, 177
Book of Common Prayer, 10
born again, 12-13, 14, 74
Brazil, Christianity in, 169
bread
  and communion, 72-73
  and Eucharist, 62
  and Mormons, 67
  and Orthodox Christians, 60, 61
  and transubstantiation, 100
bride of Christ, Church as, 55
Buddhists, 165
Bulgars, and Christianity, 17
Burleigh, Henry Thacker, 108-109
Byzantium (Eastern Roman
    Empire), 92-97, 139-142, 143,
    144, 145
  and Hagia Sophia, 94-95
  history of, 92-94
  and icons, 7, 59, 95-97, 142
  and Islam, 140
  and literature, 142
  and Orthodox Christians, 6
  as theocracy, 139-142.
  See also Constantinople

Caesar, Julius, 21, 118
calendars, 117-119.
    See also holidays

Calvary, Mount, 62, 63
Calvinism, 11, 103-105, 154-157.
    See also Puritans
Calvin, John, 11-12, 103-105,
    154-157
Campbell, Dan, 15
Canada
  Catholics in, 17
  Protestants in, 9, 17
cardinals, 7
Carey, Matthew, 79-80
Carolingian Empire, 144
Catacomb of Saints Peter and
    Marcellinus (Rome), 92
catacombs, 91-92
Catholics, 5, 7-8, 12
  and canon law, 21
  in China, 174
  and churches, 58
  and communion, 62, 63, 72,
    73
  and confirmation, 72, 73
  and conservativism, 172
  and education, 80-84
  and family, 75-76
  growth of, 17
  and Incarnation, 61
  and Mass, 57, 61-63, 70, 71,
    100
  and music, 105-106
  and Native Americans, 76-77
  and papacy (pope), 7, 8, 139,
    142-146, 153-154, 176
  and penance, 72
  Protestants versus, 157-158
  and rosary, 71
  and sacraments, 71, 72
  and salvation, 5
  size and distribution of, 7, 17,
    169, 170, 172
  and syncretism, 173
  and worship, 57, 61-63, 70-71.
  See also papacy

INDEX

INDEX

and judgment at end of world,
47
as king of Israel, 31-32
life of, 24-26, 28-30
as Messiah, 3-5, 30, 31, 32, 33,
36, 48
and miracles, 44
and parables, 26, 28, 43
and Pharisees, 23, 33, 41
and power from God or Satan,
5
and preaching about God of
love and mercy, 5
and Protestants, 9
and purity laws, 23, 24, 28-30
as Redeemer, 4
and redemption, 55
and resurrection, 5, 22, 23, 33,
42, 44
and Roman Empire, 21-24, 29,
30, 31, 36
and Sabbath, 57
and sacraments, 7
and salvation, 4, 5
and Samaritans, 28
and Satan, 38-39, 40
as Savior, 4
and Sermon on the Mount,
40-41
as son of God, 31-32
as spiritual head of Church,
143
as teacher, 23, 26, 28-29, 40,
42, 92
and world leadership, 14
and Zealots, 24, 30.
See also Gospels; Mary
Jews, 47
and anointing, 3-4
and Bible, 22, 23, 35
and covenants, 54
and Crusades, 149
and death of Jesus, 30, 36

and Easter, 119-120
and Essenes, 24
and Hebrew calendar, 118
and Jesus, 3, 4-5, 22, 23, 24,
26, 28-30, 41-42, 48, 49,
140
and Mosaic Law, 22-23, 41,
42
and Passover, 32, 119-120
and Pentecost, 127
and persecution, 161
and Pharisees, 22-23, 33, 36, 41
Puritans versus, 158
and purity laws, 23, 24, 28-29,
30
and Roman Empire, 22-24, 29,
36, 38, 41
and Sabbath, 57
and Sadducees, 22, 23, 33
and Samaritans, 28
and Zealots, 23-24, 30, 36.
See also Jerusalem Temple
Job, 52
John, 31, 135
Gospel of, 32, 38, 43-44, 49-50,
72
Letters of, 45
John, Esther, 177
John Paul II, 170, 176
John the Almsgiver, 142
John the Baptist, 43
Jonah, 92
Jones, Bob, 14-15
Jordan River, 92
Joseph, 25
Judaea, 21
Judas Iscariot, 43
Jude, Letter of, 45
judgment, at end of world, 47
Julian calendar, 117, 118-119
Julius I, 124
Justinian, 93-94
just society, 3

INDEX

Pentecost, 43, 127
Pentecostals, 13, 15, 19
  and Africa, 170
  and baptism, 15, 69
  and conservativism, 172
  and Holy Spirit, 15, 70, 127
  and prayer, 70
  size and distribution of, 172
  and worship, 66
persecution
  in American colonies, 161-162
  and contemporary Christianity,
    174-177
  and early martyrs, 133-139
  and Jews, 161
Persian Empire, Christianity in,
  16
personal holiness, and
  Methodists, 12
personal sin, 53
Peter, 30, 47-48, 143
  letters of, 45
Peter the Great, 141
Pharisees, 22-23, 33, 36, 41
Philippines, Christianity in, 169
philosophy, 3
pilgrimages, 97-98
pluralism
  and persecution of early martyrs,
    133-139
  and United States, 161-163
poetry, 89-91
Poland, Christianity in, 17
Polycarp, 135
polyphony, 102, 103
pope. See papacy (pope)
popular culture
  and African-American spiritu-
    als, 107-110
  and nineteenth-century American
    evangelicals, 110-115, 157
Portugal, missionaries and
  colonies of, 17

prayer, 57, 70-71.
  See also worship
praying-in-saloons crusade, 111
predestination, 11
Preface to the Psalter (John Calvin),
  104
Presbyterians, 8, 11-12
  and Calvin, 11-12, 103-105,
    154-157
  and education, 74
  and family, 75-76
  and Knox, 156
  and music, 104
  and worship, 104
priests, 5, 6, 7, 9, 10, 57, 70-71,
  72, 118, 153
prodigal son, 26, 43
Prohibition, 111
prophecy, and Pentecostals, 15
Protestant Reformation, 7, 10,
  151-158, 165
  and Calvin, 11-12, 103-105,
    154-157
  and education, 77, 82
  and Luther, 10, 65, 66, 101-103,
    151-154, 157
  and Protestants versus
    Catholics, 157-158
Protestants, 5, 7-13
  and baptism, 9, 73
  and Bible, 71
  and Calvin, 11-12, 103-105,
    154-157
  Catholics versus, 157-158
  in China, 174
  and church, 58, 63
  and confirmation, 73
  and conservativism, 172
  denominations of. *See* Angli-
    cans; Baptists; Lutherans;
    Methodists; Presbyterians;
    Reformed Churches
  and education, 74

INDEX

winter solstice, 124-125
Winthrop, John, 158-161
wisdom, and Pentecostals, 15
wisdom sayings, of Jesus, 26, 28
Wise Men, 124
Woman's Christian Temperance
    Union (WCTU), 110-111
women, and nineteenth-century
    American evangelicals, 110-115
work ethic, and Reformed
    Churches, 11
World Council of Churches
    (WCC), 172
world leadership, and evangelicals,
    14
worldview, 46-55
    and definition of Jesus, 47-50
    and redemption, 53-55
    and sin, 51-53
    and Trinity, 50-51
Worms
    Diet of, 153-154
    Edict of, 154
worship, 57-67
    and Anglicans, 66

and Baptists, 65
and Catholics, 57, 61-63, 70-71,
    100
elements in, 57, 58
and fundamentalists, 66
and Jehovah's Witnesses, 66
and Lutherans, 65-66
and Mormons, 66-67
and Orthodox Christians, 6,
    58-61, 70
and Pentecostals, 66
and Presbyterians, 104
and Protestants, 9, 63-67
and Puritans, 104
and Quakers, 66
regulative principle of, 104-105.
    See also music; prayer

Xavier, Francis, 175

Zaire, Kimbanguist Church of,
    170-172
Zealots, 23-24, 30, 36
Zechariah, 42
Zhiming, Wang, 177

Page:

B: © Réunion des Musées Nationaux/Art Resource, NY

C: © Elio Ciol/CORBIS

C: © Erich Lessing/Art Resource, NY

D: © Erich Lessing/Art Resource, NY

E: © Erich Lessing/Art Resource, NY

F: © Erich Lessing/Art Resource, NY

G: © Scala/Art Resource, NY

H: © Erich Lessing/Art Resource, NY

H: © Diego Lezama Orezzoli/ CORBIS

169: Chart adapted by the International Bulletin of Missionary Research, January 2003

Frontis: Chart adapted by the International Bulletin of Missionary Research, January 2003

Cover: © Elio Ciol/CORBIS

CONTRIBUTORS

ANN MARIE B. BAHR is professor of Religious Studies at South Dakota State University. Her areas of teaching, research, and writing include world religions, the New Testament, religion in American culture, and the Middle East. Her articles have appeared in *Annual Editions: World Religions 03/04* (McGraw-Hill, 2003), *The Journal of Ecumenical Studies,* and *Covenant for a New Creation: Ethics, Religion and Public Policy* (Orbis, 1991). Since 1999, she has authored a weekly newspaper column that analyzes the cultural significance of religious holidays. She has also served as president of the Upper Midwest Region of the American Academy of Religion.

MARTIN E. MARTY, an ordained minister in the Evangelical Lutheran Church in America, is the Fairfax M. Cone Distinguished Service Professor Emeritus at the University of Chicago Divinity School, where he taught for thirty-five years. Marty has served as president of the American Academy of Religion, the American Society of Church History, and the American Catholic Historical Association, and was also a member of two U.S. presidential commissions. He is currently Senior Regent at St. Olaf College in Northfield, Minnesota. Marty has written more than fifty books, including the three-volume *Modern American Religion* (University of Chicago Press). His book *Righteous Empire* was a recipient of the National Book Award.